Knowledge for the Love of God

Why Your Heart Needs Your Mind

Timothy Pickavance

WILLIAM B. EERDMANS PUBLISHING COMPANY

GRAND RAPIDS, MICHIGAN

Wm. B. Eerdmans Publishing Co.
4035 Park East Court SE, Grand Rapids, Michigan 49546
www.eerdmans.com

© 2022 Timothy Pickavance
All rights reserved
Published 2022
Printed in the United States of America

28 27 26 25 24 23 22   1 2 3 4 5 6 7

ISBN 978-0-8028-8195-3

Library of Congress Cataloging-in-Publication Data

A catalog record for this book is available from the Library of
Congress.

Unless otherwise noted, Scripture quotations are from the New International Version.

"This new book by Timothy Pickavance is like a great conversation with someone who cares about truth and faith in equal measure. It builds a convincing case for the vital importance of knowledge in the Christian life and intersperses great personal stories with needed philosophical points. Highly recommended!"

— TOM MORRIS
author of *The Oasis Within* and *Plato's Lemonade Stand*

"In this beautiful book, Timothy Pickavance shows that the free and abundant life that Jesus offers is facilitated by the life of the mind and especially by knowledge. We know many things, but what's the *purpose* of knowledge? This question sounds abstract, but as Pickavance shares his own journey and struggles as a Christian, the question becomes concretely alive and relevant. Using stories from his own life, Pickavance guides you through critical issues such as how knowledge can set you free, how we can know things apart from science, and how we can acquire knowledge from the Bible. He shows how *all* knowledge is for the love of God: both to love God and to be loved by God. For anyone seeking to go deeper in the abundant life offered by Jesus, this heartfelt book is essential reading."

— ROBERT K. GARCIA
coeditor of *Is Goodness without God Good Enough? A Debate on Faith, Secularism, and Ethics*

"This is the book I searched for in vain when my daughters were in high school and college. But now it's available, and I am so, so pleased about how good it is. Professor Pickavance has managed to put a lot of life-changing philosophical content into a conversational, easy-to-read style. It feels like Pickavance is a wise old friend sitting down to have a chat with the reader. Chock full of interesting and clarifying illustrations, *Knowledge for the Love of God* manages to drill down on one of the deepest topics facing humankind: What, exactly, is knowledge, why is it important that we gain it, and how does it relate to the love of Jesus and our pilgrimage—our real, practical, pilgrimage with him in his kingdom? Pickavance combines wisdom, knowledge, and insightful application to being a Jesus follower with an integrative approach and a warm, even funny, tone. This is now the go-to book for churches, parachurch groups, and philosophical, theological, worldview, and spiritual-formation courses in high school and college. I couldn't put it down and read it straight through! What a joy!"

— J. P. MORELAND
author of *Scientism and Secularism:*
Learning to Respond to a Dangerous Ideology

"Timothy Pickavance wonderfully avoids the traps of naïve gullibility or blind faith on the one hand and depersonalized and arrogant rationalism on the other. He ably situates the Christian faith reasonably within scientific methodology and the place of stories or testimonies, helping us rightly value knowledge in a way that both resonates with our experience and appropriately leans upon God's self-revelation. Don't apologize for the mind God gave you, but *do* recognize the strengths and limits of our reason."

— KELLY M. KAPIC
author of *You're Only Human: How Your Limits Reflect*
God's Design and Why That's Good News

"In our age of deconstruction, this timely book will benefit seekers and believers alike in reconstructing a faith that is situated on a strong foundation of grace and truth."

— DERWIN L. GRAY
author of *How to Heal Our Racial Divide: What the Bible Says,*
and the First Christians Knew, about Racial Reconciliation

For Lyle and Gretchen

Contents

CONTENTS

Foreword

When I was an atheist and legal editor of the *Chicago Tribune*, I had definite opinions about Christians. I was convinced that having faith meant that they believed something even though they knew in their heart it couldn't be true. *An invisible, all-powerful, all-loving, all-knowing creator of the universe?* Surely deep down inside they realized that this was absurd—and yet they clung to their faith because they were frightened to face the world without it.

After all, isn't there a strict division between the head and the heart? The heart is ruled by ever-changing emotions, desires, and feelings; this was surely where the idea of God resided. The mind is tethered to reality. It's fueled by facts, evidence, logic, and truth. Yet religious folks allow their heart to dominate their life, permitting their often-irrational faith to drive their worldview, attitudes, and decisions.

Or so I thought.

What I didn't see at the time was the degree to which I was letting my conclusions about these matters be ruled by my own emotions, desires, and feelings in spite of the facts, evidence, and logic pointing in the other direction.

Actually, I would have greatly benefited from the profound and practical insights that philosopher Tim Pickavance offers in this provocative book.

Is truth objective? Can religious beliefs be reasonable? Can we really know anything beyond what science can establish? What did Jesus mean when he taught that knowledge is the beginning of freedom? Can we know something because the Bible says so? With intellectual courage, Pickavance plumbs these and related topics. Through it all, we learn not just to be content with knowledge *about* God; rather, we find that our quest should be to pursue knowledge *of* God.

In an age when we're urged to "follow the science," as if it will unfailingly take us to the correct conclusions about everything from medicine to morality, Pickavance digs deep into what we can really know through the scientific method. In fact, I believe that his exploration of the limits of scientific inquiry are worth the price of the book.

As for me, my attitudes changed dramatically after my wife's conversion to Christianity prompted me to use my journalistic and legal background to investigate faith. It took me a while to get there, but I finally came to understand that biblical faith is taking a step in the same direction that the evidence is pointing. That seems logical to me.

But even after coming to faith in Christ, I haven't stopped pursuing knowledge, because as Pickavance points out, this is the pathway to truly and deeply encountering the real, living Jesus. In fact, it's the road to freedom.

Let's face it: we live in a world where truth often capitulates to tolerance; where morality is mushy; where ethical confusion reigns; and where religious beliefs are increasingly greeted with skepticism and even hostility. Today, more than ever, we need clear thinking, crisp analysis, and well-grounded answers—all of which you'll find in abundance in this short but potent volume.

So let my friend Tim Pickavance be your guide in delving deeper and deeper into how we know what we know. Oh, and you might want to keep a highlighter handy. There's much you will want to remember—and apply to your own life and relationship with God. As Jesus put it in John 8:32: "Then you will know the truth, and the truth will set you free."

Lee Strobel
author of *The Case for Christ* and *The Case for Heaven*

Acknowledgments

So many people contributed to this project. At the risk of forgetting some, I'll mention a few.

My friend and colleague J. P. Moreland has been on my case for years to write this book. If you don't like the result of this harassment, you now know who to blame! More seriously, J. P. has been an irreplaceable source of encouragement, ideas, objections, and energy. Not only that, he offered invaluable guidance and aid while I learned to navigate a new-to-me segment of the publishing world.

I wish I could inventory all the profound and unique ways in which individuals have made a difference to the pages that follow. Instead, I'll just offer my thanks to the following group: Howard and Roberta Ahmanson, Uche Anizor, Steve Bagby, Kent Dunnington, Dave and Gloria Furman, Greg Ganssle, Nicole Garcia, Barbara and Chris Giammona, Joe Gorra, Dave Horner, Heather and Ian Jacobson, Isaiah Lin, Darian Lockett, Scott Rae, Brandon Rickabaugh, Gene and Jackie Rivers, Chris and Sarah Stratton, Kyle Strobel, Lee Strobel, Gregg TenElshof, and Charlie Trimm. Tomas Bogardus, Daniel Eaton, Robert Garcia, Liz Hall, Samuel James, and Nates King and Lauffer belong in that list, but they also offered concrete pointers and tips that made their way into the book.

Of course the good folks at Eerdmans have been crucial. David Bratt, Andrew Knapp, Jenny Hoffman, and freelance copyeditor Christopher Reese each made significant contributions at different stages in the process. They have been so generous dealing with me and with the manuscript.

My students at Biola, especially the hundreds and hundreds from Foundations of Christian Thought, endured early attempts at expressing out loud the ideas in this book and walked with me as I learned how to deliver them more clearly and convincingly. In many ways, this book is for them.

My children, Lyle and Gretchen, caused me to want to write this book. Indeed, the first draft was a series of letters to them, written mostly while sitting at soccer practices. They are too young right now for what's here, so I suppose it is for their future selves. These two precious souls entrusted to my wife and me don't often get to see me working, and that means they won't naturally pick up the tools of my trade like they would if we were living in a little house on the prairie. I wish that weren't so. As I hope they know, at least in theory, my work is something I think can make a difference. I'm doing my best to help people learn to follow Jesus with all that they are and do. Someday I hope this book will be an encouragement to them as they grow into their faith, as they become adults in Christ. Anyway, I'm grateful to Lyle and Gretchen just for existing. Without them, this book would never join the world alongside them.

Three others deserve special mention. Each slogged through early, very rough drafts of what eventually became a much better book.

Molly Snelson was a willing guinea pig for the earliest version of the manuscript. Her assurance that I was at least close to the right tone and style and that nonacademic Christians just might find something valuable in these pages gave me confidence to keep going in moments when I might otherwise have given up.

My good friend Jason McMartin, also a colleague at Biola, contributed in incalculable and vital ways. He helped me bake ideas and offered fresh ones to replace those that were stale or spoiled. He supplied resources. He offered reasons to keep working. He told me to stop being an idiot when I needed to stop being an idiot. He helped me believe this book might be helpful and perhaps even *good*. I'm so grateful for his friendship.

Finally, thanks to my extraordinary wife, Jamie. She's read every word of this book, most of it more than once, all of it carefully. She gave feedback on almost every page. She is a skilled, incisive, encouraging interlocutor and editor. When I couldn't seem to move the sea of thoughts behind the book from inside my head to outside, she told me to write to my children, and the floodgates opened. When I didn't know how to solve a textual problem, she gave me ideas. She pressed me to head off objections and eliminate possible confusions; she revealed blind spots; she forced me to make choices. It would be difficult to overestimate the extent to which anything good in this book bears her mark. (Unlike J. P., she bears no responsibility for any of the remaining bad!) On top of it all, she puts up with *me*. More than puts up with me, she spurs me on toward Jesus and to fulfilling the calling that God has given to me to work on the sorts of things contained in this book. She does all this while living out the myriad ways in which knowledge is for the love of God. What a gift she is.

Prologue

CHAPTER 1

Spring 2006—Why Write This Book?

The spring semester of 2006 marked the midpoint of my doctoral program in the department of philosophy at the University of Texas at Austin. It also was plagued by interconnected personal and existential crises. Graduate school tends to exact a heavy toll, and crippling fear and anxiety are often the coin with which one pays. My debts came due in spring 2006, and I couldn't afford the fare. That semester was a pivotal one: I was to finish and defend a prospectus of my dissertation, set a committee to work with over the coming years, and thereby initiate a process in which I was meant to produce the best philosophy of my life, which would in turn secure a life in academia. But in February, a conversation with a trusted academic advisor dropped a nuke on the dissertation I had planned to write and sent me back to square one. I had two months to develop a new idea, and that first nuked attempt had taken two and a half years. I was scared of failure. But there was more. I had grown unsure whether the vocation I had committed to pursuing was worthwhile. I could no longer tell if God cared about philosophy, or at least about me becoming a philosopher. I was psychologically and spiritually spent. And even my body began to break down. I write these words at a standing desk because my back has never recovered from spring 2006. In many ways, those months brought me to the lowest point I've experienced since I started following Jesus.

But what does all of this have to do with knowledge? The short answer, which I admit is only a partial answer, is that I needed more knowledge. Certainly I needed more than knowledge, but I didn't need less. The same is true for all followers of Christ. We need more than knowledge, but not less.

⁓

I got into philosophy, and eventually into all this business about knowledge, because I wanted to help people come to know Jesus. I was convinced, rightly I still believe, that philosophers make a huge difference to what a culture takes seriously. My friend J. P. Moreland talks about this in terms of "cultural maps." The idea is that what people find plausible—what's even on the table for serious consideration—is determined by certain big-picture intellectual structures in society, and that those structures are determined, oftentimes decades earlier, by the goings-on in academic philosophy departments.[1] A big part of what philosophy departments teach a culture is what is knowable and how you can know it. (I'll have lots more to say about this later, along with examples.) Recognizing this is what made me leave the academic path I had been on previously, a path headed toward doctoral work in economics, in order to pursue philosophy. I still think what J. P. says is true, and it's reason enough to value philosophy.

What I now find troubling is that nothing in that rationale for doing philosophy answers a vital question: Why does philosophical knowledge matter for me and my children and other people in Jesus's church? Why does knowledge matter to someone once she's committed her life to Jesus? If the intellectual plausibility of Christianity is the *only* reason why knowledge is important, then knowledge is of little value once a person becomes a follower of Jesus. Maybe attending to issues of knowledge can help convince someone that following Jesus is the reasonable choice, and maybe thinking carefully about knowledge can help a culture be friendly to Jesus. But knowledge won't make a difference once you're on the Way.

Take this passage from one of the apostle Peter's letters:

> [Jesus's] divine power has given us everything we need for a godly life through our knowledge of him who called us by his own glory and goodness. Through these he has given us his very great and precious promises, so that through them you may participate in the divine nature, having escaped the corruption in the world caused by evil desires. For this very reason, make every effort to add to your faith goodness; and to your goodness, knowledge; and to knowledge, self-control; and to self-control, perseverance; and to perseverance, godliness; and to godliness, mutual affection; and to mutual affection, love. For if you possess these qualities in increasing measure, they will keep you from being ineffective and unproductive in your knowledge of our Lord Jesus Christ. But whoever does not have them is nearsighted and blind, forgetting that they have been cleansed from their past sins. (2 Pet. 1:3–9)

Peter is clearly telling us that knowledge matters for our life in Christ. But there's a way of reading this passage that suggests that the knowledge we need comes early in the process, and that most of the work is adding other things onto that knowledge. Most of us, we might think, have all the knowledge we need. What's left is to *add* the other stuff. This dovetails with the picture I had according to which knowledge really just gets us in the door. Once inside, the importance of knowledge fades.

This limited view of why knowledge matters doesn't square with certain things Jesus says, and it's not enough to flourish as a Christian in our culture, either. Which is to say, I don't think that reading of 2 Peter is a good reading. Let me explain with a story.

Throughout most of my time at the University of Texas, I commuted to campus on the 101 city bus. I exited on Guadalupe Street at West 23rd, right on the western border of UT's beautiful, dense urban campus. I made the ten-minute walk to my office in Waggener Hall, right in the heart of the hustle and bustle of the "40 acres," hundreds of times.[2] That walk took me directly past the university's Main Building. This Victorian-Gothic structure is a historic landmark of the city of Austin, and really of the state of Texas itself. The tower structure that comprises part of the building stands over three hundred feet tall, which for a very long time made it one of the two tallest buildings in Austin. The other was the Texas State Capitol, only a few short blocks away. Originally, the Main Building as a whole was the university's central library, and its tower housed the stacks of books. The architecture of the city seemed to insist that universities matter. Because knowledge matters. The building even tells you this directly. Etched in all caps into the stone facade are these words: YE SHALL KNOW THE TRUTH AND THE TRUTH SHALL MAKE YOU FREE. These are, of course, the words of Jesus, passed down to us in John's Gospel (8:32). Jesus came to offer freedom. Freedom from slavery to sin, the devil, and death. It looks like Jesus's offer of freedom is predicated on our ability to know the truth, both about and as incarnated in Jesus. Knowledge, Jesus is saying, is the beginning of freedom.

That same tower is also infamous. On August 1, 1966, from the observation deck at the top of the tower, Charles Joseph Whitman used those three hundred feet of architectural beauty and strength to his grisly advantage. For over an hour and a half, starting at 11:35 a.m., fire from Whitman's arsenal of guns rained down on the plaza below. Whitman murdered fourteen people and injured over thirty others. His bullets descended past Jesus's words.

I often thought about both of these things, ironically juxtaposed, on my walk from the bus to my office. And if I'm honest, my life reflected and still reflects both the hope of Jesus's compassionate offer of freedom and the chaos of Whitman's desperate, hopeless cruelty. In 2006, though, chaos seemed more prominent than hope. I lacked answers to vital questions. How does Jesus's path to freedom work? What is truth and where do I find it? What is it to know truth? And how in the world does knowing truth, and the truth itself, make you free? These questions don't seem to be ones many churches are interested in answering, not with any specificity. Or at least I hadn't heard the answers. I didn't yet know how to connect my intellectual life to the rest of my life with Jesus. And I've come to believe that that's part of what was wrong. My inability to answer these questions contributed to the fear and anxiety I experienced so acutely then. I was not *free*. Or at least I didn't *feel* free.

Jesus's freedom is freedom we need. It's freedom I want for my children and for my students. It is freedom from sin and death, freedom to live life connected to God, his people, and his world. This is the irony: Whitman brought death against a backdrop of Jesus's offer of life. We long to be free of the burden of sin, whether we like to admit it or not. We are, as the apostle Paul puts it, *slaves* to sin (Rom. 6:20). Such slavery is not natural for humans. So Jesus offers, in short, freedom to be *human*. And so we also need to concern ourselves with the knowledge Jesus connects to freedom. We need to know Jesus, the Jesus who is the incarnate Word, by whom, through whom, and for whom all things were made. We know this Jesus through creation, through the church, and through God's written Word, the Bible. Encounters with these things are ways of coming to know Jesus.

~~*~~

Aren't they? The culture in which my wife and I are raising our children and the culture which forms the substrate of my students' lives is not friendly to the idea of obtaining knowledge through the church or Scripture. Certainly, we as a culture believe we can know through creation—this is basically just science!—though many would not admit that creation is an invention of a *Creator*. But can we really know through the church? And through the Bible? Our culture—and if we're honest, even those of us in the church who inhabit such a culture—is skeptical that these are ways of *knowing*. Sources of inspiration? Of course. Sources of hope? Probably. Sources of belief? Why not? But sources of *knowledge*? Doubtful.

Christianity, according to this culture, is not a tradition built on knowledge. At best, we are and will continue to be confronted by voices insisting that all religions are of a piece. These voices have been around for some time. Mahatma Gandhi, for example, once said, "The essence of all religions is one. Only their approaches are different."[3] Gandhi is not alone. At worst, the voices around us tell us religion is the problem. Here's how Sam Harris put it:

> Incompatible religious doctrines have balkanized our world into separate moral communities, and these divisions have become a continuous source of bloodshed. Indeed, religion is as much a living spring of violence today as it has been at any time in the past. . . . Why is religion such a potent source of violence? There is no other sphere of discourse in which human beings so fully articulate their differences from one another, or cast these differences in terms of everlasting rewards and punishments. Religion is the one endeavor in which us–them thinking achieves a transcendent significance. If you really believe that calling God by the right name can spell the difference between eternal happiness and eternal suffering, then it becomes quite reasonable to treat heretics and unbelievers rather badly.[4]

More crudely, Howard Stern mashed the pieces together: "I'm sickened by all religions. Religion has divided people. I don't think there's any difference between the Pope wearing a large hat and parading around with a smoking purse and an African painting his face white and praying to a rock."[5]

One final point here: For many, the claim that religions are the problem is intimately connected to a claim about knowledge. Harris has been especially explicit: "While believing strongly, without evidence, is considered a mark of madness or stupidity in any other area of our lives, faith in God still holds immense prestige in our society. Religion is the one area of our discourse where it is considered noble to pretend to be certain about things no human being could possibly be certain about."[6] This felt certainty, which Harris contends is misplaced, is a central cog in Harris's argument that religion is an important source of violence and is, therefore, a problem for human culture. Daniel Dennett is more blunt: "The one thing that I think is really dangerous in many religions is that it gives people a gold-plated excuse to stop thinking."[7] Yikes.

Are Harris and Dennett right about this? Are the words of Jesus etched into UT's Main Building really a path to the slavery of death Whitman chose? Do Christian religious commitments really encourage us to stop thinking? I don't think so. In fact, quite the opposite. One central part of Jesus's ministry was to teach us how to think, and thinking well is encouraged throughout the Scriptures and has played a vital role in the church for two millennia, starting with Jesus's first disciples. But our culture, and in many ways our Christian culture, is prone to send the opposite message. We need reminders of the truth. Someday maybe I'll need them. And I want all of God's people to be equipped to give them, whether to me or to someone else in need.

None of this discussion about combating mistakes in Christianity's detractors is merely theoretical and abstract; those mistaken ideas are at best a foil for something far more important. I want my

children, my students, and the whole of God's people to experience
the insights that composed vital strands in the rope of grace that
dragged me out of the psychological morass I confronted during
my doctoral program. I want Christians to be able to answer that
question I couldn't answer when I got into this business: What
does knowledge have to do with loving and following Jesus, besides
maybe getting us through the door of God's house? I hope to supply
clarity about what knowledge is, where it comes from, and why it
matters. I also want to articulate how knowledge relates to other
important aspects of our lives, aspects like belief, truth, and faith.
And I want to connect all of that to life in Jesus's Kingdom. Part of
the task is to unearth, lay bare, and then dispel cultural myths about
knowledge and in turn the relationship between Christianity and
knowledge. Myths like the ones we've encountered from Gandhi
and Harris. More centrally, though, we need a positive vision of why
Jesus calls us to love God with our minds and why our formation
into Christlikeness relies so heavily on our minds (even if it relies
on other things, too). These are the basic tools of the life of the
mind that everyone needs—that I needed in 2006, that my children
and my students need—on the journey toward knowing the Truth
that will make us free.

~&~

With two exceptions, each chapter of this volume is ordered around
one simple question that has exercised me over the years on my
journey with Jesus. Especially so in the wake of spring 2006. Each
question is a forced choice. And the options are stark contrasts: the
way of Jesus that leads to freedom and life, and the way that leads
to slavery and death. There is no neutral party. As Jesus reminds us,
we are either with him or against him (Matt. 12:30). Will we choose
the answers that lead to freedom and life, or the answers that lead
to slavery and death?

—❧

Who is this book for?

This book is *not* for people looking for a general defense of the Christian worldview. Though I will respond to worries about the Christian faith connected to questions of knowledge, belief, faith, and so on, I am not mounting a positive defense of Christianity. This book is instead a sort of manifesto on why the life of the mind is essential for devotion to Christ. It's a book for Christians, especially Christians looking to root their faith more deeply in the Truth to whom they've already committed.

I wrote with my children, Lyle and Gretchen, squarely in mind. It is for them. But it is also for those like them whom I have the pleasure to teach, year in and year out, in my ministry at Biola University. When I look out on my classes filled with young undergraduate men and women, all I see are Lyle and Gretchen, grown up just a bit. I suppose, though, that every Christian needs what my children need. I know I did. So this book is for my children, my students, myself, and you, too.

For better or worse, every parent hopes their children don't repeat their own mistakes or suffer what they have endured. Through this book I hope to inoculate my children, my students, and indeed the whole church against some of my own mistakes, against suffering in some of the ways I've suffered. I suppose it's more than that. I don't just want folks to avoid my mistakes or my sufferings, I want to open them up to the abundant life that Jesus offers. I want to open *you* up to the abundant life that Jesus offers. And I've come to believe— to *know*, really—that abundant life is facilitated by knowledge. I want to show you how practical, and how spiritual, knowledge is. The course of a person's life is bound up with questions about knowledge. So I want to lay bare why and how knowledge is for the love of God.

Every semester I talk about these issues with large groups of students at Biola, where I've taught since before either of my children were born. Evidently, these are not things people hear about in church or anywhere else before they go off to college. In fact, every Christian hears messages about knowledge and faith throughout most of his or her life, and many of these messages push against full-throated commitment to Jesus. (I'll say something about those messages shortly.) And many young Christians never enroll at a place like Biola, where courses about these issues are required of every student. I want Christians to know these truths wherever they're educated.

I pray that this book confronts you with insights into who Jesus is and why he is so beautiful and that, in the end, these issues of knowledge and of the mind will, as the Scriptures suggest they will, bring you to deeper and more passionate worship of and communion with the Triune God of Abraham, Isaac, and Jacob.

Chapter 1 Discussion Questions

- What messages have you heard about knowledge and the life of the mind, whether good or bad? How does your church talk about these issues? (What is your church's or Christian community's attitude toward knowledge? Is it valued?) How about friends, family, teachers? Your favorite celebrities or social media personalities?

- Does learning more about God matter for the Christian life? Why or why not? Are you skeptical of the claim that knowledge matters or that abundant life is facilitated by knowledge? If so, why? What are your concerns? Be honest!

- Think about the difficult times you've had as a Christian. Do you think any of those times were connected to a lack of knowledge or understanding? If so, what do you think you were missing? What questions needed answers? If not, what was the problem?

- Does learning more about nonreligious subjects (math, bugs, literature, hockey) matter for the Christian life? Why or why not?
- What is your response to the claims of atheist thinkers like Sam Harris and media personalities like Howard Stern?
- Why are you reading this book? What are your motivations?

Part One

Knowledge

CHAPTER 2

Does Jesus Really Care about Knowledge?

My goal is to offer some tidbits about knowledge in the hopes that Christians might use them to follow Jesus more ably and more radically. The first question must then be: What *is* knowledge, anyway?

Lurking nearby is another, deeper question about why knowledge matters. Recall Gandhi's assertion that all religions are really aligned in the most important respects. And the claims of Harris and Dennett and others that religion is a serious problem for the world. Related to these ideas is the idea that one's intellectual life doesn't really matter to one's religious commitment. I said a little bit about this in chapter 1, but I'm compelled to say more. This is one of the issues I was wrestling with—not consciously, but it was there—during that crisis period in 2006.

But I'll start with a seemingly separate issue.

⁓

Here's a confession: my wife and I used to watch this reality show called *The Bachelorette* and occasionally its older sibling *The Bachelor*. I feel sheepish making this public, since folks will probably be driven to question our moral compass. I can't say I'd blame them!

Since no doubt none of the readers of this book will have ever watched even a minute of such inanity, here's how the show works. Over the course of a season, a single woman—the bachelorette—dates a group of men simultaneously. She starts with twenty-five or thirty, and through the weeks she whittles the field down, handing out roses to designate those she desires to keep on as contenders. They go on elaborate dates, all over the world, sometimes in groups, sometimes one-on-one. And in the end, after just a couple of months, she chooses one man, with the idea that he will, right then and there, get down on one knee to propose.

The Bachelorette is fascinating for a number of reasons, but I'm interested in the conscious deliberations of the bachelorettes. In every episode, the producers put the bachelorette alone in front of a camera to talk about how she's going to make her choice.

Hannah Brown was the fifteenth bachelorette, and she deliberated like every bachelor and bachelorette before her. One of the men on Hannah's season was Luke P., and Luke clashed wildly with the other contestants and in some ways with Hannah herself. But Hannah was smitten with him nonetheless. Around fifteen minutes into the fifth episode of that season, Hannah says, "The guys [the other contestants] might not understand, not get it. But Luke P. is still here because *my heart wants him to be here. My head doesn't always want him to be here.* It makes it really difficult to know what's the best decision to make. We know we have crazy chemistry, but there are red flags." Later, around fifty-six minutes into the episode, as Hannah and Luke are headed for a one-on-one date, she confesses to the camera: "I'm really excited to see Luke. But I think I have a lot of anxiety about today. There's no denying the connection that we have. There's also no denying that there are red flags . . . everywhere." She even admits around minute seventy, "I want to not like him"! So how does that one-on-one date go? It is an unmitigated disaster. Luke doesn't mollify Hannah's concerns, and in some ways he makes things worse. But guess what: Luke is still around for episode 6. Hannah's "heart" trumps her reasons for wanting to let him go. In the battle of heart and head, Hannah chooses heart.

Our culture agrees with Hannah. We oppose minds and hearts and at the end of the day go with our hearts. In these deliberations, a bachelorette like Hannah so often has all manner of reasons to choose one person but winds up ignoring those reasons and going with her "heart" or "gut." This points to a couple of things. First, we tend to think that our heart can't be swayed by what's going on in our mind. And second, we think the real guide to life is our heart, not our mind.[1]

Many churches teach, sometimes only implicitly, this heart-head conflict right alongside the culture. (Diagnostic question: does your church talk about education as an act of worship?) We downplay the life of the mind, worried about the danger of a disembodied sort of faith, separated from the world, more concerned about truth than love, failing to live out our faith in embodied ways like acts of mercy and service. This concern is well-placed in a certain sense, but I fear it misses the mark, and dangerously so. When we think this way, we wind up reasoning like the bachelorette, unmoored from facts about what's good and bad, disconnected from the great truths about God, ourselves, and morality.

The problem is that our hearts can deceive us no less than our minds. We not only love with our hearts, but we hate, too. If we indulge our hearts without ordering them with our minds, we can sow injustice and strife in our surroundings and give ourselves over to the evil within. Or if we feel nothing in particular, we simply ignore or remain apathetic. The mistake of disconnecting our minds from our hearts is disastrous. It leads us to reason about how to live like the bachelors and bachelorettes do. And therefore, when we don't feel particularly warm and fuzzy about Jesus, we don't follow him, even if we know the truth. Jesus wants something better for us!

Unsurprisingly, then, Jesus calls us to love God with everything we are and have, with our heart, mind, soul, and strength
(Mark 12:29–31; cf. Deut. 6:4–5). But, maybe most salient to the point
I'm trying to make, the Scriptures refuse the idea that our minds are
utterly distinct from our hearts. Rather, our minds are a faculty of
our hearts. Hearts are more than minds, but they aren't less. This is
the beginnings of an answer to this chapter's question. Why does
Jesus care about knowledge? Because he cares about our hearts.

Jesus was an expert in the Hebrew Scriptures—what we now
call the Old Testament. They were his Bible. No surprise, then, that
he would include the mind in his characterization of what it looks
like to love God with everything we are. The Scriptures he cher-
ished did not separate the life of the mind from life with God.

The Hebrew word translated as "heart" in the Bible is *lēb* (most
often pronounced like the first syllable of "levy"). It appears hundreds of times in the Old Testament, and usually is meant to pick
out the whole of a person. But in many cases it's more specific.
Sometimes it refers specifically to things like emotions and desires,
or what our culture would call our heart. In others it's picking out
the will (our faculty of decision-making). But more often than either emotions and desires or will, *lēb* refers specifically to the *intellect*. The Old Testament, in other words, conveys, in the very words
it uses to describe to us the idea that we cannot separate our minds
from our hearts, that our minds are as central to us as our emotions
and desires. Our heart, our *lēb*—our *self*—is more than our mind,
but definitely isn't less.[2]

To perhaps belabor this point a bit, the nuances of *lēb* are not
the only way the Hebrew Scriptures imply that hearts and minds
are intertwined. The connection between the life of the mind and
life with God is all over the pages of the Old Testament, both explicitly and implicitly. The explicit ways are easy enough to find.
Everyone should look for themselves! But here's an implicit way,

or maybe a way on the border between implicit and explicit. The story of Israel is the story of Abraham's family. That story is one that revolves around the faithfulness of God in spite of the unfaithfulness of his people. Over and over again, Israel turns away from God and toward idolatry and other sins, and over and over again God remains faithful to his people and reestablishes his relationship with them. God even has the prophet Hosea marry Gomer, who is either a literal prostitute or at least strongly inclined to promiscuity. God mandates Hosea and Gomer's union as a sort of icon of God's relationship with Israel.

Here's the thing to notice, and it runs throughout the Old Testament: Israel's unfaithfulness is rooted in her forgetfulness. God anticipates this problem. During Moses's final sermon to the Hebrews, just before his death and their entry into the Promised Land, Moses says this: "Only be careful, and watch yourselves closely so that you do not forget the things your eyes have seen or let them fade from your heart as long as you live. Teach them to your children and to their children after them. . . . Be careful not to forget the covenant of the LORD your God that he made with you" (Deut. 4:9, 23). Israel doesn't exactly heed Moses's charge. Take, for example, Israel's reaction to the death of Gideon: "No sooner had Gideon died than the Israelites again prostituted themselves to the Baals. They . . . did not remember the LORD their God, who had rescued them from the hands of all their enemies on every side" (Judg. 8:33–34). As that passage makes clear, this isn't the first time Israel forgot, and it wouldn't be the last. Forgetfulness leads to unfaithfulness.

Faithfulness is, of course, a matter of the whole heart. But forgetfulness is a matter of the mind. No doubt Israel's problems (and ours) are *more* than cognitive and intellectual. Forgetfulness of this sort is moral and volitional. It is, in short, a holistic spiritual problem. But why think that fact makes forgetfulness not a matter of the mind? Forgetfulness may involve more than the mind, but it can't involve less. So you simply cannot separate minds and hearts. There's really no space between, as Moses puts it, forgetting what your eyes have seen and letting it fade from your heart.

To repeat: Jesus cares about knowledge because knowledge is a matter of the heart. When I talk about knowledge, I'm talking about the heart. About love. We cannot deliberate like the bachelors and bachelorettes! (Incidentally, this is the first key to unlocking the mystery of what was wrong with me in 2006. More on that later.) There's much more to unpack here, and we'll get there. But first we need to delve into the issue of what knowledge *is*. To get more specific about why knowledge matters we need to understand just what we're talking about.

⁓

A distinction is in order. There are two ways of knowing to keep an eye on. One way is knowing *that* something is true. Each of us knows all manner of things in this way. My children Lyle and Gretchen, for example, know that $2 + 2 = 4$, that Jamie and I love them, that they were born and raised in Orange County, California, that China isn't the United States, that riding a bike without a helmet is dangerous, and that kicking puppies for no reason is very, very bad. All these are items of what we philosophers call "propositional knowledge." Propositional knowledge is knowledge about facts or states of the world from a third-personal standpoint. Propositional knowledge is knowledge from the "outside," as it were, in that it needn't involve any intimate or personal relationship with the thing known.

The second way of knowing is what we philosophers call "knowledge by acquaintance." It's knowledge *of* a thing that's (more or less) direct and unmediated. In this sense, my children know me but don't know Abraham Lincoln, even though they know a lot about him. Lyle and Gretchen know one another, and I know my wife and my own father, and each person knows his or her close friends. We know by acquaintance much of our own minds and wills. We even know our houses and cars and pets and favorite keepsakes in this way. But neither of my children knows my paternal grandparents by acquaintance, since both had passed away before either of my children were born. Nor do my children know the homes I grew up in or Jesus's apostles or any of the other folks they've only read about. Lyle and Gretchen might have propositional knowledge *about* these people and things, but they don't know *them*.[3]

Vitally, what God most wants for us is to know him by acquaintance. He doesn't want us merely to have loads of propositional knowledge *about* him. He wants us to know *him*. That's really what God offers us in the gospel: knowledge *of* God in all his Trinitarian glory. This is what Peter is talking about when he commands us to "grow in the grace and knowledge of our Lord and Savior Jesus Christ" (2 Pet. 3:18). Grow in your knowledge *of* Jesus, Peter says, not knowledge *about* Jesus. As it happens, I'm going to spend most of the remainder of this chapter discussing propositional knowledge. That may seem like an odd strategy! But understanding the nature of propositional knowledge is required preparation for seeing why propositional knowledge is essential for receiving the knowledge of God offered in the gospel. Acquaintance with God cannot be disentangled from knowledge about God.

꙳

Plato was an incredible Greek philosopher who was born in the fifth century BC and died in the middle of the fourth. Socrates was Plato's teacher, and Aristotle was his student. So he's sandwiched between the two other figureheads of the birth of Western philosophy, and really Western culture. Most of what we know about the thought of Socrates, in fact, we know through Plato's writings.

Plato, at various moments in his writings, was concerned with marking the difference between true belief on the one hand and knowledge on the other. For example, here's what he says in a book called the *Meno*:

> True opinions [or beliefs], for as long as they remain, are a fine
> thing and all they do is good, but they are not willing to remain
> long, and they escape from a man's mind, so that they are not
> worth much until one ties them down by (giving) an account
> of the reason why. . . . After they are tied down, in the first place
> they become knowledge, and then they remain in place. That is
> why knowledge is prized higher than correct opinion; knowl-
> edge differs from correct opinion in being tied down. (97e–98a)[4]

What's going on here? We can think of Plato's definition of knowledge as *reasonable true belief*. In other words, Plato is suggesting
that in order to *know* that something is true, we have to believe it,
it has to be true, and we have to have good reasons for believing
it's true.

Here's an illustration. My children both know that I love them.
So if Plato is right, three things must be the case. First, it has to be
true that I love them. I can attest to this, so that's settled. Second,
each of them has to *believe* that I love them. A person just can't know
something without believing it. And both Lyle and Gretchen do
believe that I love them. And third, they must believe this about
my love *reasonably*. Reasonableness is a bit more complicated, but
the basic idea is that you have good reasons or evidence, or a solid
foundation for, your belief. I'll discuss the myriad ways you can get
this sort of thing in chapter 4. But in this case, Lyle and Gretchen
have rather overwhelming evidence for their view that I love them.
I tell them both that I love them, and they both know that I'm not
prone to lying. (Gretchen used to get playfully annoyed by me
telling her I loved her over and over again, especially just before
bedtime.) And I hope I've shown them both over the years that I

love them as well and in lots of different ways. I mean, I've endured both Disneyland and Pictionary *just for their sakes.* These various evidences are appropriate ways to observe and experience love, and as such, they provide a solid foundation for my children's belief that I do, in fact, love them both. So Lyle and Gretchen believe a truth in a reasonable way. That's knowledge!

What Plato said has influenced and informed hoards of other thinkers over the last 2,500 years. Take Dallas Willard. Willard was a philosophy professor at the University of Southern California, which is all the more impressive in light of the fact that he made significant contributions to the renaissance of attention to spiritual formation in evangelical Christianity. That's not something most USC philosophers care much about! According to Willard, knowledge is "the ability to represent a respective subject matter as it is, on an appropriate basis of thought and/or experience."[5] That's a bit of a mouthful, but it aligns nicely with my Plato-inspired characterization. The *belief* part of our definition is captured by Willard with "represent[ing] a ... subject matter"; the *truth* part is captured by "as it is," and the *reasonable* part is contained in the bit about an "appropriate basis of thought and experience." I'm planning to say more about this three-part formula as I proceed. But reasonable true belief is enough for now.

That's the short story about what propositional knowledge *is.* I don't take myself to have given any real argument that this is what knowledge is. (I could do that, but it's important to see that I haven't even tried.) I do think the testimony of folks like Plato and Willard should carry some weight all on their own. Anyway, most of the points of tension among philosophers concern fine details and nuances that are necessary to really get the account of knowledge absolutely perfect. So they're best left aside. None of those details and nuances will make much difference to the ideas I'm concerned with here.

Jesus cares about knowledge because knowledge matters. One way
knowledge matters is that we act according to what we take ourselves
to know. When you're deliberating about whether to do one thing
or another, you're considering the consequences of your actions,
which is to say you're considering what you and your surroundings will be like depending on which way you choose. Take a silly
example. You're at a birthday party, and there are cupcakes. You've
already had one, and you're thinking about whether to have another.
You might think, "Well, if I have another, I'll get to enjoy another
cupcake, so that's good! On the other hand, it might make me feel
sick, and that's bad! Then again, it might not." The idea is that you
know you'll enjoy it, but you don't know whether you'll feel sick.
Usually, the knowledge that you'd enjoy another cupcake wins out
in deliberations like this. You'll probably take another cupcake!

Obviously there are more serious cases than whether to eat a
second cupcake at a birthday party. Maybe you're on a jury deliberating about some serious crime. Maybe you're trying to decide
whether to keep dating someone. Maybe you're wondering whether
to take a job offer. Who knows? But the point will stand: knowledge
ordinarily wins out in our deliberations. If you know that something
is true, you'll ordinarily take that thing for granted in your deliberations and decision-making. In that way, you act on what you know.
Likewise, the more uncertain you are that something is true, the less
likely you'll be to act on it. That's one reason knowledge matters: it
filters down into our actions.

My concern, though, is deeper. It's with why Jesus would care
about all this intellectual stuff about knowledge. It can seem dry
and irrelevant to really important issues like love, and anyway it's
hard to get good at knowing. It's just a lot of *work*. So why bother?
This question is especially pressing in light of the fact that what
God really wants for us is acquaintance with him. It turns out that

the reasons to care about knowledge are actually quite clear in the Scriptures. They reveal that knowledge is anything but dry and irrelevant and that the hard work of knowing is very much worth it. The short story about why knowledge matters is that knowledge prompts and supports worship and grounds our formation into Christ followers. The flip side of this is that sacrificing and suppressing knowledge, ignoring the life of the mind, leads us to idolatry and character deformation.

My 2006 self didn't grasp these connections. I can't explain why just yet. To make good on these claims about how knowledge relates to Jesus following, and to relate that to my own experience as a Jesus follower, we first must work through this reasonable-true-belief thing in a little more detail. I'll start with the issue of truth.

Chapter 2 Discussion Questions

- Were you surprised by the idea that the Bible situates the mind within, rather than opposed to, the heart? Do you tend to view the mind and the heart as connected, or do you tend to make a distinction between the two?
- How is knowledge connected to love, or how are the head and the heart connected?
- What is the difference between propositional knowledge and knowledge by acquaintance? Can you think of examples of each?
- Can you think of a time when your heart deceived you?
- Has forgetfulness ever caused you to hurt a friend?
- Why does Jesus care about knowledge?

CHAPTER 3

Is Truth Objective?

Jesus said, "If you hold to my teaching, you are really my disciples. Then you will know the truth, and the truth will set you free" (John 8:31–32). I mentioned this passage already, back in chapter 1. The last bit is graven into the facade of the Main Building at the University of Texas. But it's the first bit that I'm interested in here: "If you hold to my teaching..." That and something Paul says in Romans 1:18, that people "suppress the truth by their wickedness."

During the summer of 2006, coming off that wretched spring semester, Jamie and I went on a five-week trip to England, France, and Italy. We had various friends to stay with (for free!) in Portsmouth on England's southern coast, in London, in a little town called Tiehet near Toulouse in the South of France, and in Florence. Those free stays with friends made visits to the Lake District in northern England, Paris, the Cinque Terre, and Rome possible as well. It was incredible.

I couldn't enjoy that trip to the fullest because my beloved Dallas Mavericks were making a deep run in the NBA playoffs, and I wouldn't be able to watch the games. I had been a Mavs fan since the late 1980s, and for the vast majority of that time they were terrible. But in 2006, the all-time-great Dirk Nowitzki, flanked by a young group of talented players like Josh Howard and Devin Harris and Marquis Daniels, made an incredible run to the finals. Their opponents were the Miami Heat, featuring Shaquille O'Neal, who not long before had won three straight championships with the Lakers, and Dwayne Wade, one of the more dynamic shooting guards in recent NBA history.

The 2006 NBA Finals was, and still is, controversial. Wade attempted twenty-five free throws in game five, as many as all Mavs combined. The Heat overall went to the line an astounding forty-nine times in that game. Wade took ninety-seven free throws in the six-game series and averaged over eighteen free throw attempts in the four games after the Mavs went up two games to none. Ninety-seven free throws is a record in a six-game NBA Finals and eclipsed Shaq's ninety-three in 2000. But in that 2000 NBA Finals, Shaq was being *intentionally fouled throughout entire games* because he was such a terrible free throw shooter. About the game five free throw disparity, Bill Simmons, former ESPN commentator and in no way a Mavs fan, quipped, "I just don't see how there's any way this can happen in a fairly-called game. It's theoretically impossible."[1]

Why were—are?—Mavs fans so enraged? Because they were convinced that Dwayne Wade was getting phantom foul calls. In a fair game the referees call fouls when there is a foul and don't call fouls when there is no foul. The fouls themselves should precede and dictate the referees' judgments. Good refereeing consists in rightly recognizing fouls and calling a foul precisely because a foul has occurred. To miss fouls that have occurred, or, as with Wade, to call a foul when none occurred, is to referee poorly or unfairly.

This outrage is about truth. It assumes that there is a fact of the matter about whether a foul occurred, and that this fact is independent of what anybody, including the referees, think or believe. The job of the referee is to rightly recognize fouls. And the foul call is an expression of a particular judgment: the judgment that a foul has occurred. This judgment can be true or false, depending on whether a foul actually occurred. We might put the point this way: referees don't *make* a foul a foul, they *call* a foul a foul.

Whether a foul occurred is, in this sense, an objective matter. Given that the rules of basketball are what they are, it matters not what we think or believe. A foul either occurred, or it didn't. In Wade's case, many of the foul calls happened when there was no foul! (Maybe I'm still more a fan than I thought . . .) The calls were, objectively, inaccurate. They were false.

Similarly, there are all manner of things we believe about the world that are objectively accurate or inaccurate, true or false, right or wrong. In believing, we represent the world as being a certain way. And those beliefs are true or false insofar as they represent the world accurately or inaccurately. Just like NBA referees, we don't *make* the world with our beliefs, we *call* it. The rules of basketball are taken as given for NBA referees in that the referees don't make the rules by making their calls. Likewise, the world is taken as a given in our beliefs. Our beliefs don't make the world.

I want to add, and emphasize, that the idea that our beliefs don't make the world requires a good bit of nuance. A full accounting must happen elsewhere, but I do want to admit that there are lots of ways that humans shape reality. We make art and corporations, we make promises and decisions, we form teams and governments and games. Our beliefs—about aesthetics, economics, morality, practicality, sport, and society—are part of that shaping, in that what we believe will affect what we do, and what we do shapes the world. But that is compatible with the claim that our beliefs don't make the world in the sense I intend. First of all, each of these ways that we shape reality *presuppose that there is a reality that is absolutely independent of us.* Even an artist needs raw materials; they cannot create, as only God can, out of nothing. Similarly, the idea of a basketball foul requires the prior existence of human bodies, facts about contact between human bodies, and so on. These realities are absolutely independent of human beliefs. Even historical facts about human decisions relevant to the creation of the rules of basketball are not dependent on present human beliefs. Second, and relatedly, those ways that we shape the world make objective changes to reality. Given what we've objectively done to objectively shape the world, the world is objectively one way rather than another. Whether a particular basketball action will objectively be a foul in the future is something we can change through collective choices and activities. But we can't change whether something is foul *just by believing*. Our responsibility in believing is to match our beliefs to the reality we encounter.

During that trip to Europe in 2006, the NBA Finals were a nice distraction from the deeper troubles I should have been wrestling with, troubles about my life and future with Jesus. Perhaps surprisingly, those troubles were intertwined with the finals via this idea of truth.

⁓✦

Since I devoted my life to Jesus in late December 1996, I've not wrestled significantly with whether Christianity is true. I have, though, wrestled with what it means to *say* that Christianity is true. What I mean is that I've sometimes struggled to remain confident that religious claims are like foul calls: judgments about a reality independent of me. It can be tempting to think that our beliefs about religion are less about truth and more about producing certain feelings of purpose or contentment or satisfaction, or whatever it is we want deep down.

This isn't really a surprise. There is a strong current in our culture to treat religious truth fundamentally as an instrument of progress rather than as an accurate representation of reality. The question whether religious beliefs are "true" is really the question whether they *work for you.* This is why, for example, Gandhi and many others are able to get away with, and even be praised for, saying that all religions are really one. All religions are simply ways to achieve a better self. They aren't, in any deep and meaningful way, about a reality independent of us.

Looking back at the way I was approaching my life and the world around me in the spring of 2006, it's fair to say that I had imbibed this perspective at a level that was perhaps subconscious but that had important practical relevance. This is not to say I wasn't a Christian. I had entrusted my life to Jesus. And if you had asked me, I would have said that the central claims of Christianity were true. I was engaged in a Christian way of life. And when I panned out and considered the big picture, I thought Christianity was capital-T True.

But—but!—I also was convinced that the truth of Christianity, and my commitment to the God of Christianity, meant that my life should *work* in a certain way. That I should be more or less free of struggle and my life free of strife. And that I should, to be blunt, get my way. When the blows came—the crippling fear and anxiety about the future—I lacked the resources to square my experience with what I believed was the truth. One source of that inability, though in no way the only source, was a particular conception about what it meant to say that Christianity was true.

The thing is, I knew even then that Christianity was fundamentally about past, present, and future realities, realities I couldn't control or manipulate, that don't turn in any way whatever on what I desire, feel, or long for. Either God created everything apart from himself or he didn't. Either God chose Abraham, Isaac, and Jacob or he didn't. Either Jesus is God or he's not. Either Jesus was crucified or he wasn't. Either Jesus rose again or he didn't. Either Jesus ascended into heaven and sits at the right hand of the Father or he doesn't. Either Jesus is my High Priest or he's not. These are not at all claims about what works. They are claims about what *is.*

I must conform myself to these realities. They do not, nor could they, conform to me. We must "hold to [Jesus's] teaching" so that we might "really [be his] disciples." He is the teacher, and our role is fundamentally to embrace the truths he delivers. The way these truths "work" is secondary to whether they simply *are*.

The idea that I must conform to reality rather than conform reality to me is at odds with two deep, persistent currents shaping our cultural waters. The two currents are modernism and postmodernism, which have their own characteristic views of truth and its relationship to humanity. These two currents, though distinct, press in a similar direction. Both push us toward the idea that we must shape reality to our own ends. Surprisingly, those currents are twisted byproducts of the underlying source of the sea itself, the first moment in the overarching story of reality: God's creation of the world. In the case of modernism, the twisting comes by disrupting the next two stages in the story of reality, the Fall of the world into slavery to sin and death and the redemption of the world in Jesus Christ. In the case of postmodernism, the twisting comes by severing the connection between creation and the Creator himself. Both put mere humans into a position only God can rightly occupy.

I should unpack that a bit.

—⚓—

Take modernism first. Modernism is both a movement and a period of time, spearheaded by a diverse group of European, British, and American thinkers tracing from around the middle of the sixteenth century through the end of the nineteenth. There are no hard-and-fast end points here. But it's fairly common to mark the beginning of the modern period with the publication of Nicolaus Copernicus's world-altering cosmological vision, with the sun at the center of things, in 1543. And many mark the transition from modernism to postmodernism with the towering figure of Frederich Nietzsche, who died in 1900. The Scientific Revolution of the seventeenth century, starting with Copernicus and ending with Newton, was the catalyst of the development of distinctively modern philosophy. And the Enlightenment of the eighteenth century, starting with Newton and ending with the French Revolution, was in many ways modernism's crowning achievement. Both were explosive epochs, and they share the same heart. Dramatic advances in mathematics and science brought with them a technological revolution. And, not unrelatedly, dramatic upheavals in philosophy and theology emerged as well. Modernism is in no way monolithic, but we can identify a strand of thought that characterizes the modernist view of truth.

Modernism rightly confesses that truth is objective. Something is true when it accurately represents the independent reality of the world. Sometimes people will express this by saying that truth is correspondence to reality. That's what modernism gets right. There are two troubles, however. The first is that the modern mind refuses to reckon with the way the Fall disrupts our access to the truth and thereby fails to appreciate the need for divine grace in our knowing. The second is that the modern mind is convinced that the world's ills can be overcome by humanity alone and thereby fails to appreciate the need for divine grace in our redemption. The first trouble makes space for the second. If we rightly see our need for divine grace in knowing, we're encouraged to view the tastes of heaven that come by way of human ingenuity as ultimately coming from God as well.

René Descartes was a French mathematician, scientist, and philosopher who laid the philosophical groundwork for the modern period. He was a contemporary of Galileo, a generation or two after Copernicus. Descartes himself would be the first to tell you that he was a revolutionary. In a fantastic book called *Descartes' Bones*, Russell Shorto relays that Descartes "was after the kind of philosophy that would take the world by the throat, that would make the people 'the lords and masters of nature.'"[2] That last bit, about being lords and masters of nature, comes straight from Descartes's own *Discourse on Method*. Here's the bit of Discourse 6 Shorto is talking about:

> A practical philosophy can be found by which, knowing the power and the effects of fire, water, air, the stars, the heavens and all the other bodies which surround us, as distinctly as we know the various trades of our craftsmen, we might put them in the same way to all the uses for which they are appropriate, and thereby make ourselves, as it were, masters and possessors of nature. Which aim is not only to be desired for the invention of an infinity of devices by which we might enjoy, without any effort, the fruits of the earth and all its commodities, but also principally for the preservation of health, which is undoubtedly the first good.[3]

As Shorto puts it, "Descartes became convinced that he would crack the body's code and extend the human life span to as much as a thousand years."[4] Royals around Europe were on the edge of their seats, looking to Descartes to preserve them and, thereby, their rule. And Descartes was clear that progress was not to be found in "the Schools," that is, the philosophy of the church.

Contrast Descartes's optimism with what God says in Genesis 3: "Cursed is the ground because of you [Adam]; through painful toil you will eat food from it. . . . It will produce thorns and thistles for you. . . . By the sweat of your brow you will eat your food until you return to the ground" (3:17–19). God disagrees with Descartes. God says we will face toil because of Adam's sin, and because of the sin we inherit from Adam. Descartes places his hope in human technological achievement to escape the effects of the Fall. God offers us the hope of resurrection life through the person of Jesus. Not technology, but love made possible through grace.

Further, Descartes fails to reckon with the pernicious effects of the Fall on our access to the truth. As Os Guinness puts it, "As human beings we are by nature truth-seekers; as fallen human beings we are also by nature truth-twisters."[5] We will distort the truth to serve our ends. No surprise that the technological advancement Descartes foresaw has had alarmingly negative consequences alongside the astoundingly positive ones. Descartes and his followers wrought modern medicine and atomic bombs, democracy and fascism.

Couple these two modernist mistakes—overconfidence in humanity's abilities independent of God, and a failure to reckon with the Fall—and the modern mind aims to conform the world to our own desires by sheer technological force.

Earlier I asserted that modernism was in no way monolithic. Yet postmodernism may somehow manage to be even less monolithic than modernism. The postmodern mind is a product of a reckoning with the scientific image of reality produced through the modern project. Reality, according to full-throated modernism, is just a collection of very tiny things chaotically bumping in an ultimately meaningless void. In the wake of Darwin, humanity too is squarely situated within this story. We are nothing more than collections of tiny things produced by mindless, random, chaotic bumping of other tiny things. Nietzsche, who lived around a generation after Darwin and who embraced this vision with clear-sightedness, recognized that this picture utterly abandons any vision of how humanity ought to live. This is why Nietzsche marks the turning point between the modern and the postmodern. Postmodernism is a reaction to the chaotic wake of the modern scientific image of the world.

In the face of this kind of chaos, the postmodern instinct is to insist that truth and meaning are constructs of human communities. There is no objective reality to represent in our minds and in our language. We make meaning in community together, and in this way we make truth, too. We, together, create the world. Because there are different "we's" there are also different truths. In this way, truth is relative, constructed variously in community and for community.

The postmodern mind, however, is also cognizant of all the technological progress we've made. As a result, very few are thoroughgoing constructivists in the sense I described in the previous paragraph. Usually, postmodern people are modernists about physical reality and relativists about things like morality and religion. I want to return to this division shortly.

Others have made the case against the postmodern conception of truth and especially of the relativism that accompanies it. No point in repeating here what they say so well.[6] But I want to add to the chorus of voices my agreement on two fronts. First, relativism and constructivism are self-defeating if applied wholesale. Each is inconsistent even with itself. Take relativism. If relativism is true, then there are no absolute truths. But that means relativism isn't true! Second, relativism about good and evil, which is both an inescapable consequence of thoroughgoing postmodernism and a characteristic feature of many more limited forms of postmodernism, is both unlivable and repugnant. You would rightly protest if someone took your belongings without permission or if someone helped themselves to your body without your consent. There is simply no doubt that the Cambodian killing fields and police violence against innocent African Americans are expressions of evil. And there is no doubt that personal sacrifice on behalf of the vulnerable is good.

God demurs from this postmodern vision. "In the beginning, God created the heavens and the earth." The world was made prior to us arriving on the scene. So it cannot be up to us what it is ultimately like. By setting mere humans up as creators, postmodernism severs the connection between creation and the Creator. Such severing is unacceptable. Only God is Creator.

To wholeheartedly embrace modernism or postmodernism is to embrace one of two ways of "suppressing the truth" (Rom. 1). Modernism and postmodernism align in insisting that we, rather than God, are masters of reality. We are creators, not he. We are saviors, not he. In this way, both embrace a form of idolatry wherein humans occupy the role of Creator, which is rightly God's alone. Fundamentally, as Paul continues on in Romans, this is about what we will worship. Will we worship the Creator, or will we worship the creation?

—⸙—

I want to return briefly to the postmodern division between objective truth in the physical realm and constructed truth in the religious realm. Christianity, as I've already hinted, has no patience for this division. The central message of the gospel hinges on a claim about history, and history falls on the objective side of this division. The gospel, therefore, drags the religious back into the objective world, whatever anyone says.

This is crucial because, whether or not there are aspects of reality that are constructed by human communities, Christianity is— objectively—either true or false. According to Christianity, God creates and sustains the whole of reality independent of him, and we are a part of that created order. God, therefore, is not a human construct. He precedes and underlies human communities, and so cannot be constructed by them. God's existence is objective. Likewise the other central tenets of Christianity. Either Jesus is God incarnate or he isn't. Either he was crucified or he wasn't. Et cetera. You might think about it this way. The fundamental facts about historical events are objective, and since Christianity is rooted in history, the truth of Christianity is objective as well.

Therefore, all the theological, moral, and practical claims that follow from the central Christian message are likewise either objectively true or objectively false. What follows from something objective is itself objective. The main contours of the Christian vision of reality—the Christian "worldview"—are objectively true or objectively false. To say that Christianity could be true for one person or community but not for another is to say that Christianity is false for everyone. Christianity simply has no space for that sort of relativity.

Gandhi, on this score, was just wrong. And self-actualization, moral formation, and all the other great stuff that might go along with religious commitment must take a back seat to the simple question of whether Jesus was who he claimed to be and whether he did what Scripture says he did. As Paul puts it to the Corinthians, if Christ did not rise from the dead, then our faith is futile (1 Cor. 15:17). I was wrong to assume that part of what made Christianity true was its working in a particular way in my life. Christianity is not primarily a way to be happy or healthy. It is primarily a set of claims about reality. It is true no less for the Hindu or the Buddhist than it is for the Christian. In light of this, we must conform to the world—ordered fundamentally around the gospel of Jesus—rather than conforming the world to ourselves. This point alone couldn't kill the spiritual and existential crisis that began for me in spring 2006, but it certainly cuts one of the roots.

Tragically, Christianity won't "work" for the Hindu or the Buddhist (or adherent of any other non-Christian creed) in the long run. They all deny the truth essential for experiencing the eternal peace of God, both in the present life and in the life to come. God may give grace, in the myriad forms his grace takes, to anyone he desires. "He causes his sun to rise on the evil and the good, and sends rain on the righteous and the unrighteous" (Matt. 5:45). But the eternal peace and joy that comes from abiding in the presence of God is available only to those who know where to find God and what it takes to dwell in his presence.

We're beginning to venture near to what knowledge is for. But there's more to say before we can address that adequately.

Chapter 3 Discussion Questions

- Have you ever been burned by a referee making a bad call? How objective is the rule that governs the call that referee made?
- Are there objective truths about religion, morality, beauty, fashion, and cuisine? How can we tell?
- Have you felt like the Christian life should work a certain way and been discouraged when it hasn't? What truths from Scripture do you need to tell yourself in those moments?
- What questions do you have about the difference between modernist and postmodernist conceptions of truth?
- Where do you see echoes of modernist of postmodernist ideas in public discourse, in advertising, or in social media? What about in your education up to this point?
- What does it mean to say that truth is objective, and why think that it is objective in that sense? Why does it matter that Christianity is objectively true?

CHAPTER 4

Can Our Religious Beliefs Be Reasonable?

In the middle of his gospel, Mark tells a rather typical story of Jesus's earthly ministry.[1] Jesus's disciples were trying and failing to heal a young boy of demonic possession. His father was desperate. He'd watched his son be thrown into fire and water by the demon, whose intent was to destroy the boy. He begs Jesus, "If you can do anything, take pity on us and help us." Jesus's reply is sharp: "'If you can?'" If?! This man does not understand who Jesus is, and Jesus's question likely hit the man square in the chest. No doubt he was worried he'd ruined his best chance to find healing for his beloved son. Jesus continued on, "Everything is possible for one who believes." The story resolves—because of course it does—with Jesus's mercy on display, the demon defeated, the boy healed. But what's striking to me is the father's reaction to hearing Jesus say that everything is possible for those who believe. The father's exclamation is immediate, as if he'd already recovered from the bruising rebuke a moment earlier: "I do believe; help me overcome my unbelief!"

I believe. Help my unbelief. This father says this right to Jesus's face, and Jesus doesn't turn his back on him. Instead, he gives the man his deepest desire: the rescue of his beloved son.

If you'd asked me in May 2006 what my deepest desires were, I would have listed a few: a thriving marriage, a happy family, and a job as a philosopher. The point of the last chapter is that I believed but needed help with my unbelief as well. My anxiety, my stress, were born—in part, not wholly—of unbelief, of a failure to fully embrace the goodness of God, which makes all things possible. Unlike the boy's father in Mark 9, however, I had not seen clearly my unbelief.

That's the sort of thing that people often talk about when they talk about this story from Mark 9. Rightly so. But I'm interested in a different issue. What did the boy's father mean when he asked for "help"?

Presumably, the boy's father wanted Jesus to give him something that would diminish his unbelief in a way that respected and took seriously the roots of that unbelief. What I mean is that there are humane ways of modifying and shaping a person's mind, and there are inhumane ways of doing that same thing. We all know, deep down, the difference between education and manipulation, between teaching and brainwashing, even if we can't say exactly in what the difference consists. A big part of the difference, though probably not all of it, is that in education the pupil is respected as a rational creature, and the tutor endeavors not only to deliver the truth on some matter, but to deliver it in a way that allows the pupil to understand, to see for herself. In manipulation, the rationality and personhood of the subject is not respected in this way. They are simply an experimental subject or a pawn in a game, to be molded in some way to serve some sort of end they didn't choose. Hopefully that helps you see what I mean when I say that the boy's father wanted Jesus to deal with his unbelief in a way that took seriously unbelief's roots. He wasn't asking to be manipulated or brainwashed. He was asking for education.

Jesus actually gave the boy's father the help he asked for. Jesus performed an action, right in front of the man's face, that rendered continued unbelief unintelligible: Jesus healed the boy. By healing the man's tormented son, Jesus confronted the father with the reality of Jesus's authority and trustworthiness. Continuing to disbelieve in the possibility of healing and the power of Jesus was simply not an option. Not because Jesus brainwashed him, but because we're all rational enough to see the truth when it confronts us in such a clear way. The father simply couldn't continue in his unbelief.

It must have been something like what we Cubs fans experienced during the 2016 World Series. All of us were, to some degree, disbelievers about the Cubs. We believed, but also disbelieved, that the Cubs would win that series. Even during game seven, my disbelief waxed dramatically when Rajai Davis bombed that two-run, game-tying homer off Aroldis Chapman in the bottom of the eighth. I thought there was no way back. But then rain came. The Cubs regrouped. They took the lead in the first frame of extra-innings. And when I saw, with two outs in the bottom of the tenth, the ball fly from Kris Bryant's hand to Anthony Rizzo's glove at first base, disbelief was no longer possible. My eyes were not brainwashing me; I was being educated. The Cubs won the series.

—❦—

I want to elaborate on all this, since it will aid us in understanding the nature of knowledge. If knowledge is reasonable true belief, and truth is accurate representation, then two central questions remain. First, what is belief? And, second, what makes a belief reasonable?

For our trip to England in June 2006, Jamie and I bought a rail pass. We had planned a trip to the Lake District in northern England with our friends Jo and Rob and a day trip to Winchester, Hampshire, so that Jamie could introduce me to the Winchester Cathedral and to a bench under a droopy tree at the edge of a little pond at Hyde Abbey, a bench that had been a sort of retreat for her during a

semester she spent in London. Jamie let me choose what to do with
the final day of our rail pass. As an aspiring philosopher, I chose Oxford. For someone raised in Texas, Oxford feels ancient, and that age
somehow carries a kind of weighty importance, like the pale stone
walls contain the memory of the thousand years of Oxford's history.
We stumbled across the University Church of St. Mary the Virgin,
which sits adjacent to the Radcliffe Camera, a bizarrely cylindri-
cal neoclassical building originally designed to be a science library.
St. Mary's has a tower that is open to the public, and we climbed
to the top and took in the crowds of Gothic spires that mark the
corners of the various colleges that compose Oxford University. As
we climbed back down the tower's staircase, we decided we may as
well have a gander at the interior of St. Mary's. As we scanned the
room, I looked to my right and saw a man sitting, reading. My first
thought was, judging just from the top of the man's head and the
shape of his shoulders, "That looks like J. P. Moreland."

That thought made me pause. I hadn't thought of J. P. in some
time; we hadn't talked in a couple years, actually. But he had been
my first philosophy teacher, and we had written a paper together
that became my first academic publication. J. P. had been a mentor
to me, and a guide really, during the early years of my journey as
a philosopher. Given my psychology at the time, anxious as I was
about the future, it was comforting to be reminded of a friendly
philosophical face and of early successes I'd had. Jamie and I remained stationary for a beat or two, just long enough for the man
in the pews to pause his reading and raise his head.

It became quite clear why the man *looked* like J. P.: he *was* J. P.
This was a shock. We didn't know he was in England, and he didn't
know we were there either. But somehow we wound up in the
same place, at the same time, thousands of miles from either of our
homes. He recognized me. I smiled and shrugged. He dropped his
gaze to his feet and shook his head with joking disappointment. The

three of us wandered around the streets of Oxford talking about what was going on in our lives, about the challenges I'd been facing. I didn't understand then, though it's clear to me now, that this was in fact the head of the trail toward a faculty position at Biola. God was on the move to give me the thing I feared I would never get.

Even as it was happening Jamie and I sensed something of the miraculous in this experience. And it was deeply encouraging. We still believe this seemingly chance encounter with an old friend and mentor was in reality God caring for us. God showed us his involvement in our lives. He showed us that he saw us and mercifully orchestrated for us to see him, too. I believed even then that God cared for me, but I needed help with my unbelief. And God came through (even if he came through later than I would have liked). In other words, God was convincing me, and my wife too, of deep and important truths about himself and his world, not by manipulation but by education.

God showed his care for us by giving us *evidence*, just as Jesus did for the boy's father in Mark 9. This is an important aspect of how God deals with our unbelief. He doesn't manipulate us into a change of view. Rather, he *educates*. This brings us back around to knowledge, to reasonable true belief. I'd like to camp out on the *reasonable* bit of this formula. I'd like to say something about what makes a belief reasonable, which very much has to do with evidence.

─❦─

It is, however, impossible to say what makes a belief reasonable without saying something about what a belief *is*. I won't pretend to offer some philosophically adequate definition or account of belief. That's okay, though, since belief is something everyone is already acquainted with. So what I really want to do is help you get your mind directed toward certain states within you, and to notice some differences between the mental states of interest to us in this chapter and some others that reside in the same neighborhood.

Some of what's going on in your mind describes your view of the world, your understanding of reality, what you *take to be true*. These happenings are your beliefs. Belief in this sense is a way of representing reality as being a certain way. (There's another sense of belief that I'll mention in a bit.) Your beliefs describe the things you take to be in the world and the way those things relate to one another. Your overall set of beliefs is sort of like a mental map of the whole of reality. Individual beliefs are more specific: they represent some aspect of reality as being a certain way. The particular way a particular belief represents reality is the *content* of that belief. You might believe that God exists, that $2 + 2 = 4$, that Minecraft is fun, and all manner of other things. These beliefs differ in their content. It's because of their content, *how* they represent things to be, that beliefs can be true or false. If a belief represents accurately, it is true. If a belief represents inaccurately, it is false. If you believe that God exists then you believe truly, since God really does exist. Likewise if you believe that $2 + 2 = 4$, since $2 + 2$ really does equal 4. For all of us, some of what we used to believe is false (and in fact we gave up those beliefs precisely because we discovered that they were false). For example, my daughter Gretchen once believed that the tooth fairy existed. Now she knows better: that belief was false.

Beliefs aren't thoughts, though the two categories are related. Thoughts are similar to beliefs in a certain sense, since thoughts are descriptive like beliefs. But thoughts needn't be endorsed. You can have a thought that you eventually reject. You might, for example, think, "Maybe I should root for Arsenal instead of Tottenham." And then you would of course immediately reject that idea as ridiculous, since Arsenal is the absolute worst! That is, you can consider the truth of some claim in thought without believing that the world is as your thought describes it as being. In thought, you *consider* what reality might be like. In belief, you *endorse* that reality is in fact that way. Thoughts, then, are more transient, more temporary, than beliefs. Beliefs tend to stick around in your mind, at least for a while. They are sort of like endorsed, standing thoughts. The language we use to talk about this stuff is tricky, by the way. Sometimes, for example, we use "think" as a way of saying what I would here mean by "believe." That's okay, so long as we're able to distinguish the different mental goings-on one from another. (Don't confuse the *language* we use to describe reality for the reality being described!)

Desire is different from belief, too. Desire concerns how you *want* the world to be, not how you take it to be in fact. We all know what it's like for our desires to be frustrated. This is just reality failing to match our desire. Maybe you desire to be rich and famous. This is very different from believing you're rich and famous. Same with fear, longing, hope, and all sorts of other mental states. You can fear that a bear is going to break in to the house without desiring or believing or hoping for that to happen.

These different types of mental states—belief, thought, desire, fear, hope, and so on—can have the same content. The content of these mental states are propositions (which I mentioned in chapter 2). Our minds are able to relate to the same content in different ways, and that's what marks the difference between the belief that a bear is going to break into the house and the fear that a bear is going to break in. Same content, different mental *attitude* toward the content.

Just to be explicit: I assume we all, every one of us, are already acquainted with these differences. Everyone has beliefs, thoughts, and desires, and all of us know how to tell them apart. I'm just trying to point out the differences and to supply some language to talk about these various mental happenings.

~*~

I mentioned already that beliefs can be true or false and that they can also be reasonable or unreasonable. This latter difference is going to turn on questions of evidence. We want our beliefs to be true, since we navigate the world according to the mental map constituted by our beliefs. But we don't always have immediate or direct access to the truth. We get at the truth via *indicators* of the truth, via aspects of the world that point to other aspects. This is just the idea of evidence. Evidence points toward the truth. And by gathering evidence, we get pointers toward realities we can't access immediately or directly.

A belief is reasonable when we either access the truth of the content of that belief immediately or directly, or when we have high-quality evidence that points to the truth of the content of that belief. Here are some examples. Sam is our family's giant schnoodle, a mix of a giant schnauzer and a standard poodle. His full name is Samwise MadEye DogFaceDog. He's pretty big. Weighs around seventy-five pounds, with a very hard, very thick skull. Recently, my son Lyle was crouched on the floor playing with Sam when both lunged for a ball at the same time, and Sam headbutted Lyle right on his forehead. Sam was, of course, unfazed, but the encounter caused significant discomfort for Lyle. He believed, in that moment, that he was in pain. And his belief was reasonable. Obviously so! Why? He had immediate access to the pain and thereby to the truth of the content of his belief that he was in pain. He didn't need evidence that he was in pain, something independent of the pain that points to the reality of the pain. He could just tell immediately. This is true of many (but not all!) of our mental states. Therefore, many of our beliefs about what's going on in our own minds are reasonable, even though we don't have evidence that points to their truth. (Lyle couldn't produce evidence that he was in pain, but he still knew it to be true.)

Other beliefs require evidence. These days, my family often plays this game, the "Animal Game," at dinner. Lyle invented the game, so far as I recall. It's pretty simple, and here's how it works: someone picks an animal, and then other people ask yes-no questions to try to figure out which animal the person is thinking of.

It's animal-only Twenty Questions, without the twenty-question limit. When we first started playing, Gretchen wasn't particularly reliable at knowing the answers to the questions we'd ask about the animal she chose. So she'd whisper her animal to Lyle, and he, using his encyclopedic knowledge of the beasts of the world, would help answer Jamie's and my questions about whether the animal was a mammal, or lived in the sea, or was only found in South America, or whatever. Gretchen used Lyle to point to the truth about these things. His testimony was for her, and for us really, evidence. She didn't have direct access to the truth about these issues like she does about much of what's happening inside of herself, and so she used pointers to the truth. She used evidence.

Both avenues to reasonable belief—immediate access and evidence—relate to truth. That's key. Truth is what we're after (it sets you free!). Reasonableness ties our mental representations of reality, our beliefs, to the truth, whether directly or indirectly. Evidence is valuable when we don't have immediate access to the truth because it ties our beliefs to the truth. Evidence, in this way, links our beliefs to the truth. That's the value of evidence.

Where we get our information about the world, therefore, matters. The more often a source of information indicates the truth, the more evidential value that information has. Lyle is a shockingly reliable storehouse of information about the animal world. He's a source of high-quality evidence about animals. On the other hand, horoscopes are a terrible source of information about the future. The claims of some random horoscope has no evidential value whatever. What about the *Los Angeles Times*, or *The Economist*, or NPR? Happily, we don't have to settle those questions. But this I can say: how much evidential value these sources of information provide is a function of how reliable they are at pointing us to the truth.[2]

—❦—

There are two important questions here. Where do we get good evidence? And how can we be confident that those locations are supplying good evidence? I want to make a start on these in a moment.

First, though, one bit of clarification is in order, with a promise. The clarification: there's another sort of belief. The type of belief I've been talking about is the sort of belief we talk about when we say that we believe *that* God exists, believe *that* 2 + 2 = 4, believe *that* Minecraft is fun. This is sometimes called *propositional* belief. The other sort of belief we talk about using "belief *in*." You can believe *in* God (to be faithful), believe *in* your parents (to accept you without condition), believe *in* your friends (to keep their promises). This kind of belief is really just *faith*. It's propositional belief—belief *that*—together with trust *in*. The promise is that we'll return to the issue of faith (chapter 5). Here, I simply want to forestall confusion between the two.

Back to evidence. Traditionally, Christians have distinguished two broad sources of evidence, often labeled general revelation and special revelation. General revelation includes areas of study like physics and chemistry, biology and psychology, and even philosophy. Special revelation includes the voices of prophets and Jesus, and the Bible. Both of these forms of revelation, according to the Christian tradition, are sources of information authored by God himself. They are both ways that God speaks. That is the sense in which they are both forms of *revelation*. God is revealing things about himself and about the world in "general" and "special" ways. The difference concerns, primarily, the audience of the communication. The audience of general revelation is, well, *general*: it is directed to all people at all times and places. It is generally available. The audience of special revelation is typically much narrower, usually God's people, or some section of God's people, but almost always a specific group in a particular time and place.

Special revelation is what we normally think of as God speaking. In fact, many Christians, especially those within evangelicalism, think just of the Bible when they think about God speaking. And the Bible is indeed one form of special revelation. But there are others. For one thing, the person of Jesus—the whole person!—is special revelation. When the author of Hebrews says that God "has spoken to us by His Son" (1:2), he or she means that Jesus's person and life, not just his words, are prophetic speech from God. This makes the point the author of Hebrews presents in the opening line of the letter, that God has spoken "at many times and in various ways" (1:1). The primary form of special revelation is, then, Jesus himself in both word and deed. But special revelation takes other forms, like prophetic speech, dreams, and, centrally, the Bible.

You can see the sense in which various bits of special revelation have a "special" audience by noticing that different books of the Bible are written in the first instance to a particular group of people. Deuteronomy, for example, was in the first instance a sermon of Moses to the Hebrews as they were about to enter the Promised Land. Ephesians, on the other hand, was a letter from Paul "to God's holy people in Ephesus, the faithful in Christ Jesus" (1:1). This is not to deny that these parts of the Bible are not in an important sense *also* written to the whole church, to each individual Christian and to the whole body collectively. It's just to emphasize that the audience is not, in the first instance, universal.

General revelation, on the other hand, is God speaking through the created order itself to everyone, not through appointed spokespersons to a particular group. General revelation is what we listen to when we do science or mathematics or philosophy. It is how God reveals the world to us through the power of the human mind put to work on what we see and experience and intuit about the world and the way it works. This is why general revelation has the audience it does: everyone has access to the created order. Everyone

can, if they have the time, energy, and resources, do science and
mathematics and philosophy. Different individuals may experience
different roadblocks to receiving general revelation. Those roadblocks might be material or psychological or social or cognitive. But
among the roadblocks will not be that God did not include them
in the relevant audience.

When we engage in these forms of learning—that is, when we
listen to God speak his general revelation—we are studying patterns in God's mind and will. We learn about the world but also
learn about God himself. What a great gift!

To reiterate, both general and special revelation are forms of
revelation. They are both modes of divine speech, ways that God
communicates truth to us, his creatures. General revelation is not
independent of God in any meaningful way. It is just as much a form
of divine communication as special revelation. We see this most
clearly in the way general and special revelation unite in the Word
of God, the Son, Jesus Christ. The apostle Paul communicates this
beautifully in his letter to the Colossians:

> The Son is the image of the invisible God, the firstborn over all
> creation. For in him all things were created: things in heaven
> and on earth, visible and invisible, whether thrones or powers
> or rulers or authorities; all things have been created through
> him and for him. He is before all things, and in him all things
> hold together. And he is the head of the body, the church; he is
> the beginning and the firstborn from among the dead, so that in
> everything he might have the supremacy. (1:15–18)

Paul is asserting that Jesus Christ, as the divine Word, is above and
beneath and behind of the whole created order. It's being made
"through him and for him" means that it speaks both to who he is
and to what he is doing. Here there are echoes of John's Gospel,

which teaches that Jesus is the Logos—the Word, the "ordering principle"—of creation, and of Hebrews, which says, "The Son is the radiance of God's glory and the exact representation of his being, sustaining all things by his powerful word" (1:3). The source of creation is God himself, and creation's nature and structure teach us about God. "The heavens declare the glory of God," the psalmist says (Ps. 19). Creation also makes declarations about itself. But this is only because God, and in particular Jesus Christ, is behind it all. Therefore, insofar as the created order gives us information about itself and about God, that information is ultimately coming from God. Good evidence indeed!

Notice, though, that Paul (and the author of Hebrews) slides so easily from general revelation to special. Because Paul sees both as ultimately having their source in Jesus Christ, there is no need to keep them apart or to oppose them. Paul can confidently assert that we learn through what is revealed in creation and also that we learn through what is revealed through God's prophets. Ultimately, both trace back to Jesus, who is one with the Father and so is God himself (John 10:30). This is why we can be confident both that "all truth is God's truth," as the great Arthur Holmes put it, but also that both general and special revelation are sources of high-quality evidence about God and his creation. Both are forms of divine speech. And where God speaks, we ought to listen.

Further, we *need* both forms of revelation. God has chosen to communicate to us in these two modes, and each contains parts of the story of the world that the other does not. We can't learn calculus or the atomic composition of various elements by reading the Scriptures. But we can't learn the path to restoring our relationship to God by doing mathematics or science.

This is not to say that general and special revelation never answer the same questions. Sometimes they most certainly do. We can, for example, learn about history by doing archaeological digs, reading letters from long-dead witnesses, and studying artifacts passed down through the generations. But we can also learn about history from reading the Scriptures. We should be open to communication from God wherever and however he chooses to communicate. And he quite clearly has chosen to communicate about some subjects in multiple ways. All the better for us: more of God's voice to hear!

I'll have more to say about general and special revelation down the road. There are important ways that our culture misleads us about these sources of evidence, and I want to display those mistakes in the hopes that we'll avoid them. For now, I just want to emphasize one thing: to allow God to educate us about himself, his plan, and his world, we must open ourselves to what he is revealing, both inside and outside the Bible. God is not a liar, and he desires to help your unbelief as Jesus helped the father of the demon-possessed boy we encounter in Mark 9. He wants to *show* us the truth that will make us free. But we need eyes to see, and a willingness to listen. God will not always drag us halfway across the world to confront us with important truths about himself, but he is always speaking, and will always supply what each of us needs (even if not what we thought we needed, or in the manner we would have liked). Listening to God speaking, through both general and special revelation, is how we get evidence and, thereby, reasonable belief.

~&

But who cares? Why does it matter that we have reasonable belief, especially in the realm of religion? Well, first, because knowledge is what sets us free, and knowledge requires reasonable belief. That just pushes the problem back a step; it doesn't tell us why reasonable belief is related to freedom. Reasonable belief brings freedom in no small part because we act on what we believe confidently, and typically, the more reasonable your belief, the more confidently you believe it. And look, Jesus and his first followers said some fairly ridiculous-sounding things. He and they tell us that to find your life you must lose it, that power is perfected in weakness, that you cannot earn God's favor, that you shouldn't worry about tomorrow. And then they tell us to order our lives around these bizarre claims. We're told that the life we long for is found in a life that *acts* on these truths.

Here's the thing about humans, though: we naturally order our lives around what we take to be true. Not too long ago, there was a big dustup about a commercial airliner, the Boeing 737 MAX 8. A couple of these planes had crashed in fairly rapid succession, many precious lives tragically lost. Boeing initially insisted that the crashes were just terrible accidents, but as time went on it became clear that there was a flaw in the planes' navigation equipment that was behind the crashes. Boeing eventually admitted as much. That's already horrible, and a nightmare for a company who asks people to trust that their planes are safe. But it got even worse. Over time, it became clear that Boeing knew. They knew that there was a problem and didn't say anything about it. When I get on a plane, and especially when I take my children with me, I do so because I believe the plane is safe, that there are teams of people checking and quadruple-checking that all will be well over the course of the flight. I no longer trust Boeing to tell me the truth. So I am now far more skeptical of the safety of Boeing airplanes and therefore far more cautious about boarding a Boeing plane. Boarding a plane is an action, and it's one that we perform only if we confidently believe certain things to be true. It's only because I'm confident that people not affiliated with Boeing are ensuring that Boeing planes are safe that I would be willing to travel on a Boeing aircraft. That makes sense, of course, because the stakes of the action are really quite high. It's life or death.

This fact, that we act according to how confident we are, applies all the more when the stakes level up. And make no mistake: when it comes to reckoning with Jesus, the stakes are as high as they can be. What he promises is either a life better than life or a death worse than death. If we are to follow him faithfully, we must believe what he says—even the things that seem ridiculous—with confidence. Happily, God gives us the evidence we need, through the Scriptures and through the created order.

Importantly, though knowledge requires confidence founded on good evidence, it does *not* require perfect confidence. There's an old tradition, dating back hundreds of years, according to which knowledge requires more than just reasonable belief, that knowledge requires *certainty*. What I mean is that, according to this tradition, a person can't know something if she isn't certain it's true, if the evidence she has is even possibly misleading. This is far too demanding a standard, for it would mean we don't know much of what we fairly obviously *do* know. For example, sometimes my vision is misleading, but I can still know there is a computer in front of me. Sometimes I'm wrong about the contours of my emotions, but I know I have great affection for my wife and children. Sometimes I make calculation errors, but I can still know that I did my taxes correctly. Knowledge doesn't require certainty.

I don't mean to suggest that one cannot have faith in Jesus while lacking confidence. However, following Jesus into the fullness of the life he promises is going to be exponentially more challenging without that confidence. In an emergency, if I had no other options, I might still get on one of those 737 MAXs, but I'm definitely looking for alternatives first. Faith in Jesus is possible in the midst of tentative belief, but rational confidence is something we should seek. And that's going to require attending to the evidence Jesus gives us. We need Jesus to educate us.

We're not told what happens to the father of the demon-possessed boy in Mark 9, nor do we know what happens to the boy. The story is really about the difficulty of dealing with the demonic, and so ends with a conversation between Jesus and his disciples about why the disciples couldn't heal the boy themselves. But my guess is that the boy and his father didn't walk away and forget about their encounter with Jesus. They had both been dealing with a death worse than death, and Jesus brought them into a life better than life. The transition was undeniable. So I suspect they lived out their earthly days in confident recognition of Jesus's love and power, and that their lives reflected what they knew about Jesus. If I'm right, the truth they encountered that day changed their lives forever.

Jesus's care for Jamie and me on that daytrip to Oxford in June 2006 changed us, too. The change manifested slowly—maybe it's still manifesting!—but things were never the same for us. Speaking just for myself now, the taste of God's providential care for us that day brought to life passages like the one from Mark 9. I've gained more from the stories of Joseph and Moses, of David and Ruth, of Mary and Peter, and of all the other biblical heroes and heroines whose encounters with God's redemptive care gave rise to devoted lives through confident belief in God's person and character. The evidence was there all along, but I'm now able to *see* it, as it were.

Here is a prayer I often pray, echoing the father who met Jesus face-to-face:

Lord, I believe. Help my unbelief. Educate me where I fail to believe what is true and where I mistakenly believe what is false. Show me the truth about you, about me, and about your world. And do this so that I might follow you with confident abandon. For your glory and, through your glory, my good.

Chapter 4 Discussion Questions

- Make a list of different types of mental states. How would you describe or characterize each type? Do your descriptions differentiate them from one another?
- Where do you go when you have a question? What sources of information do you trust?
- How confident are you that you can know that Christianity is true?
- When in your life have you seen God endeavor to "educate" you? Where do you need God to educate you?
- Are your religious beliefs reasonable? Why do you believe what you believe?

Part Two

Knowledge and Life with Jesus

CHAPTER 5

Is Faith Compatible with Knowledge?

My main area of philosophical expertise is metaphysics. I've published a good many articles and books on questions about the most general aspects of reality, questions like, "What is the nature of time?" and "How is it that the world might be different than it is?" and other quite abstract issues like those. One of the courses I teach every year at Biola is a graduate-level class on metaphysics. Recently, I filmed that class so that people could take it online who couldn't move to California to take it with us in person. I start the class by talking about why metaphysics matters and why, especially, it matters *now*.

The short story is that metaphysics matters because traditionally philosophers have thought that how you ought to live is in very large part a function of what sort of thing you are. If each human really is a creature made by a loving God in the image of God, then we have a special role to play in the created order, as bizarre as that might seem. This role to play, this purpose for our lives, should order how we live. But if we are instead just collections of atoms swarming in a purposeless void . . . well, the way we ought to conduct ourselves is almost certainly very, very different. The history of philosophy displays these connections in fascinating ways. A few

hundred years ago, the dominant philosophical view of humanity (at least in the West) began to shift from the creature-with-a-
purpose view to the collection-of-atoms-in-a-void view, and this
has made a huge difference to the way we as a culture think about
the right way to order our lives. As much as I'd like to go on about
this progression, this book just isn't the place.

As I was preparing to film the lectures for my metaphysics class,
I was rereading a book by a French philosopher named Luc Ferry,
looking for helpful insights and quotes to use in a lecture on why
something as seemingly arcane and abstract as metaphysics might
really, truly matter. The book is called *A Brief History of Thought*. It's
worth a read. I returned to Ferry's book because he sets up the story
of philosophy in a helpful way, given my goals for my opening lecture.
Ferry thinks of philosophy as the search for a theory of salvation, a
story that makes sense of our experience and that ultimately helps us
deal with the facts of human brokenness and death. I remembered
thinking during my first reading of the book that I didn't like Ferry's
discussion of the relationship between religion and philosophy. The
second read didn't disappoint. I only had to get to p. 6 to find the
trouble I was hunting. Ferry maintains a stark contrast between philosophy and religion. Roughly—this is a bit of a simplification, but
one that makes no difference to the point I want to make—religion
depends on God to bring salvation to humanity, whereas philosophy
is humanity's attempt to find salvation independently from God,
using just *our* reason and *our* resources. Here are some of Ferry's
own words: "Unable to bring himself to believe in a God who offers salvation, the philosopher is above all one who believes that by
understanding the world, by understanding ourselves and others
as far our intelligence permits, we shall succeed in overcoming fear,
through clear-sightedness rather than blind faith."[1] Seeing as how I'm
both devoted to Jesus and a philosopher myself, I have some quibbles
with this characterization. I'll come back to this.

Not long ago, I picked up a book called *Early Christian Martyr Stories*. It was written by Bryan Litfin, who spends his life studying these kinds of things. The stories are crazy, and mostly horrific. And they span centuries of the church.

Here's one.

Vibia Perpetua of Carthage was born into an aristocratic family in the late second century AD in Roman North Africa. At the time, Carthage was an impressive city, a center of trade and commerce thriving on grain and olive oil. It was arguably the second-most important metropolis in the western half of the Roman Empire, second only to Rome itself. Perpetua's aristocratic heritage matters for two reasons. First, life for aristocrats in Carthage at the time was, in Litfin's reckoning, "sweet."[2] Second, Perpetua's noble upbringing meant she was educated and therefore literate, and some of her writings have survived the centuries between her and us. Not long after Perpetua's death, maybe within a generation, the letters she wrote while imprisoned for her faith were collected together by an editor and annotated with accounts of the events surrounding those letters. The letters, together with the account of the editor, witness to Perpetua's final days. This is what we know.

In AD 203, when Perpetua was twenty-two, not long married, and nursing an infant son, she was arrested and imprisoned. Her crime was simply her faith in Jesus, expressed publicly in her baptism, which functioned as the final step along the way to full membership and participation in Christ's church. Public baptism, however, was unacceptable to Rome. Eventually, Perpetua was thrown to wild beasts in Carthage's amphitheater, surrounded by two crowds, one of other martyrs and the other of bloodthirsty onlookers. In the arena, Perpetua was trampled by a cow, only to rise to redo her hair so that she would not look as though she were "mourning in her moment of triumph."[3] In the end, she had to be killed by the sword. The editor's recounting of Perpetua's final earthly moments is jarring: "Perpetua shrieked as the sword was thrust between her bones. Then she herself guided the young and inexperienced gladiator's wavering hand to her throat. Perhaps we might say that such a great woman . . . couldn't be killed unless she herself allowed it."[4]

What's striking about Perpetua is the manner in which she approached her doom, not just in those final moments, but throughout the ordeal. She seemed to embrace her death, as if her earthly life paled in comparison to her devotion to Jesus, as if she really believed Jesus when he said that those who wish to find their life must lose it (Matt. 10:39). Her father repeatedly pleaded with her to recant her Christianity to avoid the otherwise inexorable execution. Even before she was baptized, while still just under house arrest, her father intervened:

> My father earnestly tried to dissuade me with words and kept seeking to break my resolution out of his great love for me.
> "Father," I said, "Let me give you an example. Do you see this vessel lying here, this little pitcher or whatever?"
> "Yes, I see it," he replied.
> "Could you call it by another name than what it really is?"
> "No."
> "It's the same with me. I can't be called anything other than what I am: a Christian."[5]

What does this mean, really? It means that Perpetua had faith that God had called her to follow Jesus, no matter the cost. She had embraced the reality of Jesus and was willing to embrace the division of family that he promised (Luke 12:51–53). As she inched toward her death, Perpetua had numerous opportunities to recant. Each time she refused. She could have escaped her death and returned to a comfortable aristocratic existence. Perpetua refused and instead sacrificed herself for her beloved Savior.

Juxtapose Ferry's contention that faith is blind, opposed to clear-sightedness, and requires putting away our reason with what Perpetua chose to endure because of her faith. Dwell on that for a bit. I hope the juxtaposition strikes you as odd. But *why*? *Why* is it odd?

⟶

Centrally, the oddness stems from the fact that we act on what we take ourselves to *know*. This is something I've already discussed, and I don't want to dwell too long on it now. But it's really quite clear that we don't do things, especially important things, painful things, and things that are both important and painful, unless we believe deeply and confidently that the belief we're acting on is true.

Please don't hear what I'm not saying. I'm *not* saying deeply and confidently held beliefs are always rational. It's certainly possible to have beliefs that are both utterly irrational but held deeply and confidently. We can believe deeply and confidently without good reason! But set that atypical possibility aside. First, we've already seen (in chapter 4) that religious beliefs can be reasonable. Second and more importantly, cases of utterly irrational, deeply and confidently held belief are simply not what I'm addressing here. I'm also not saying that every martyr is acting on knowledge. But—and this is crucial—the failure of knowledge is just as likely to be a failure of *truth* as of *rationality*. I think, though I don't have space to defend, that the vast majority of believers in false religions and ideologies have at least minimally rational beliefs (in the sense of rationality in play on these pages). They believe on the basis of misleading or incomplete evidence. They fail to know not because they are irrational but because their beliefs are *false*. And what a tragedy it is to give your life away or to commit heinous acts on behalf of falsehood. The good news is that Christianity is *true*. So Christians can't fail to know because their beliefs are false.

Back to the main plot. I'm not talking about atypical cases of utterly irrational but deeply and confidently held belief. I'm talking about the legitimate connection between belief and action. We act on what we confidently believe, and normally that means we act on what we know.

So I think Perpetua *knew* that God would care for her in the end, and this knowledge is what gave her the courage to face such a gruesome death. She certainly needed more than knowledge to withstand the horrors she endured. No doubt she had bravery and resolve. But there's no way she could bear up under torture unless she *knew*. Just no way. As Pope John Paul II puts it in his encyclical *Fides et Ratio* (that is, *Faith and Reason*), "The martyrs *know* that they have found the truth about life in the encounter with Jesus Christ, and nothing and no one could ever take this certainty from them. Neither suffering nor violent death could ever lead them to abandon the truth which they have discovered in the encounter with Christ."[6]

Martyrs *know*. This is not blind faith. This is faith born of knowledge. We need more than knowledge, not less.

⚓

It's unsurprising, then, that when you actually consult the Scriptures, they put faith and knowledge together. There isn't a hint of a conflict between the two. Think about the opening of Luke's Gospel: "I . . . decided to write an orderly account for you . . . so that you may know the certainty of the things you have been taught" (1:3–4). Or 1 John 3:2: "We know that when Christ appears, we shall be like him." There's more where those came from. Indeed, the Scriptures are rather obsessed with knowledge. There's talk of knowledge all over their pages. (More on that in the next chapter.) In light of this consistent message about the importance of knowledge, we already have reason to expect that faith and knowledge will flow together.

Helpfully, God gives us even more to go on. For example, the Bible simply doesn't contrast faith and knowledge; instead, it contrasts faith and sight. In his second letter to the Corinthians, for example, Paul says that "we are always confident and know that as long as we are at home in the body we are away from the Lord. For we live by faith, not by sight" (5:6–7). But maybe that doesn't give us the insight we're hoping for. Here's a longer passage from earlier in that same letter:

> But we have this treasure in jars of clay to show that this all-surpassing power is from God and not from us. We are hard pressed on every side, but not crushed; perplexed, but not in despair; persecuted, but not abandoned; struck down, but not destroyed. We always carry around in our body the death of Jesus, so that the life of Jesus may also be revealed in our body.... It is written: "I believed; therefore I have spoken." Since we have that same spirit of faith, we also believe and therefore speak, because we know that the one who raised the Lord Jesus from the dead will also raise us with Jesus and present us with you to himself. All this is for your benefit, so that the grace that is reaching more and more people may cause thanksgiving to overflow to the glory of God. Therefore we do not lose heart. Though outwardly we are wasting away, yet inwardly we are being renewed day by day. For our light and momentary troubles are achieving for us an eternal glory that far outweighs them all. So we fix our eyes not on what is seen, but on what is unseen, since what is seen is temporary, but what is unseen is eternal. (4:7–18)

What an encouragement when you're hurting, and we all hurt sometime during our lives in this broken creation. In this respect, it's helpful to remember all that Paul went through. You can read about his travails in Acts, and also his report in 2 Corinthians 11. He knew suffering, and he could still call it "light and momentary troubles" (2 Cor. 4:17). How could he do that? Notice two things that for some time I missed. The first is that Paul claims to *know* the truths that define his hope. *We*, Paul says, *know* that we will be raised from the dead like Jesus was raised. And remember, this is good news! That resurrection means eternal life with our loving Father in the bliss of the new Eden. I'll come back to the second after I mention another passage.

Hebrews 11 beautifully describes what faith supplies for us:

> Now faith is confidence in what we hope for and assurance about what we do not see. . . . By faith we understand that the universe was formed at God's command, so that what is seen was not made out of what was visible. . . . All these people [great heroes of our tradition] were still living by faith when they died. They did not receive the things promised; they only saw them and welcomed them from a distance. . . . By faith [Moses] left Egypt, not fearing the king's anger; he persevered because he saw him who is invisible.

The author of Hebrews moves fluidly between faith, understanding, assurance, perseverance, and a way of life. It's amazing what faith in the living God brings. Far from contrasting or opposing faith and knowledge, Hebrews ties them intimately together.

I threatened to make a second point about 2 Corinthians 4. You might have noticed something in those passages: faith gives us more sight than we would otherwise have! Moses *saw* him who is invisible. This flies directly in the face of the cultural view of faith which asserts that faith requires closing yourself off to evidence and, thereby, to reality. On the contrary, God tells us that the eyes of faith can see things unavailable to ordinary eyes. As Paul says, it is by faith that "we know that the one who raised the Lord Jesus from the dead will also raise us with Jesus." How? Because by faith we are able to "fix our eyes . . . on what is unseen." The confident belief that enables us to act faithfully even in the midst of grave trouble is not irrational confidence, it is confidence bred from knowledge of the unseen world, engaged by the eyes of faith.

By faith, we *know*. Let that settle in your heart's mind. Faith supplies knowledge we would otherwise lack.

⟶֎

What, then, is faith in God, according to the Bible? It's not believing without evidence. Rather, it's believing (whether for good evidence or not) and trusting put together. It's belief *in*. Faith is not opposed to knowledge. Nor does it require it. It's possible to have faith in something when the belief that in part makes up your faith is irrational or unreasonable. In that case, you have an irrational or unreasonable faith. It's also possible to have faith that is rational or reasonable. This happens when your faith is constituted by a rational or reasonable belief. The rationality of faith is determined by the rationality of the belief constituting it.[7]

Faith, belief *in*, is actually quite mundane, and needn't be religious. It's the sort of thing we can have in all manner of things, from rocks and bets, to schools and businesses, to ourselves and our friends, and even to God. My family makes a habit of criss-crossing the country during the summer on sometimes excruciatingly long road trips. When we started doing this consistently, our road trip car was a 2015 Ford Flex. We bought it new in late 2015. In the summer of 2016, we made two long trips, one to Texas and another to Seattle. For the trip to Texas, Jamie was visiting a friend in Portland for a few days, so Lyle, Gretchen, and I set off without her toward my dad's house in Fort Worth. Jamie would fly to Fort Worth directly from Portland. I woke both kids up around 5 a.m. on the day we left and plopped them in the car for the first leg, a fifteen-hour trek to Albuquerque. None of us were worried about whether our car could make the trip. Indeed, we knew it could. It was almost brand new, and the V6 engine Ford uses in the Flex is a trusty, known commodity that has been a Ford staple for a long time. There was no reason to worry. So we had faith that the Flex would make it. We trusted our car. Indeed, we trusted precisely because of our knowledge. Our faith was rational.

Examples like this are easy to multiply. Here's one more. My family loves In-N-Out Burger. When we've eaten there, not once have I wondered whether a booth seat will hold when I sit down. I've never thought to check a booth's structural integrity, to test it for weaknesses, or to pay someone to be my booth tester. I just walk over and sit. This is an expression of faith in the booth, and perhaps also of faith in In-N-Out to maintain their restaurants. No doubt you could construct examples of your own along the lines of cars and booths.

Cases in which faith is betrayed, in which the object of faith lets someone down, are no doubt possible. All of us have likely witnessed someone sit in a trusty chair only to have it collapse under them, chuckled at video of a "trust fall" gone wrong, or driven past a driver staring forlornly at a smoking hood. These are possible, but they are atypical. That these cases are atypical is, I'm willing to wager, born out in your own experience. Everyone has had more successful miles in a car than disastrous ones, more chairs that have held under their weight than have collapsed.

Nonreligious faith, like our faith in our Flex, can pretty obviously go together with knowledge. And there is no meaningful difference between these kinds of faith and religious faith. In fact, a central sort of faith that we have throughout our lives is faith in other people. My children have faith in one another and, I hope, in their parents. We have faith in them to tell us the truth and care for one another, among other things. They have faith in their friends, as do we, and we all have faith in our local church to care for us if our lives go sideways. All of these faiths we have are well-founded.

They are constituted by things we reasonably believe, that is, by knowledge. We know they'll tell us the truth; we know our church will come through for us; they know their friends are faithful. Religious faith, at least Christian faith, is analogous to this. It is faith in the person of Jesus Christ to follow through on his promises. That's really all it is. So we have yet another path to the idea that faith and knowledge are compatible.

One last point. Sometimes, far from being irrational to *have* faith, it's actually irrational to *lack* faith. When Lyle and Gretchen were young, they were in the same multi-age classroom at a local elementary school. Either Jamie or I would almost always deliver them more or less to the door of their classroom. This meant driving to the school, which was not in our neighborhood, parking a couple blocks away, and walking from the car to the campus. That process took some time, which, given that both Jamie and I are generally conscientious about being on time to things, usually wasn't a problem. But one day Jamie was running later than normal, and that meant that in order for the kids to avoid being tardy, she needed to drop them closer to the school than she could park and have the pair of them walk together to the classroom. Lyle was, to put it mildly, not enamored with this plan. He's never been one for trying new things, especially if he doesn't know well in advance that the new thing is coming for him. In this case, his resistance to the idea was amplified by his lack of faith in himself. He simply didn't believe that he could do it without his mom. He lacked faith in himself to get to the school, which was only a block away, with other parents and children peppering the sidewalk along the way, many of whom knew him and Gretchen by name. And here's the kicker: Lyle was more than capable of following through with this, even as young as he was. Jamie and I knew it, too. We knew he could do it. We knew he was conscientious, smart, and cautious. This is why Jamie was willing to trust him to walk himself and his precious little sister to school. And he knew this, too, and thereby should've trusted himself. If Lyle ever reads this, I hope he won't take what I'm about to say the wrong way: *he* was the irrational one in this story, not his mom. His lack of faith was irrational, and his mom's faith was rational.

⁃

Therefore, when Ferry and others assert that religious faith is blind, it can't be because it's *faith*. (Even if that's what they're actually thinking!) What I mean is that the fact that religious faith is *faith* can't alone justify the claim that it's blind or irrational. It's not in the very nature of faith itself to be irrational. Rather, those who charge religious faith with irrationality must already believe that there's no good reason to have the religious beliefs that are constitutive of religious faith. That is, they must believe that there is something about religious belief as *religious* belief that is irrational, or maybe arational. This, in turn, makes the faith constituted by that belief an irrational kind of faith.

Are they right about this? We've already seen some reasons for thinking that's not true. But there is more to say. In due course, we will turn to three common worries one might have that Christian belief, and therefore Christian faith, is unreasonable, that Christian belief can't amount to knowledge and therefore that Christian faith really is blind. The first worry is that you can't know something without the aid of science, and science hasn't verified Christianity. The second worry is that you can't know something just because the Bible says it's true, and distinctively Christian belief is formed primarily on the basis of the Bible. The third worry is that you can't know something when lots of smart and well-meaning people disagree with you, and there are lots of smart and well-meaning non-Christians.

These are among the questions I've been wrestling with since I started reflecting seriously on the central claims of Christianity. For different reasons, some to do with my own experiences in life, some to do with serious intellectual question marks, I was for a very long time torn about whether the Christian worldview could withstand these challenges. I doubt I'm alone, and my hope is that the insights that have helped me navigate these murky, choppy waters might help others as well.

I'll get to those issues in Part III. For now, I hope you'll reflect on the way that knowledge supports faith as well as on the way that faith expands knowledge. I also hope you'll read some of those martyr stories. They're moving, even if horrifying. And they serve as a sign of what Christians can endure when they draw near to God.

Chapter 5 Discussion Questions

- What examples of mundane faith can you identify in your own life? (No chairs or cars!)
- How convinced are you that religious faith is analogous to more mundane examples of faith? Can you think of any important differences, especially differences grounded in the Bible?
- Why does it matter that faith and knowledge can go together? Is this a new idea to you? If so, why might you be reluctant to see the two connected?
- Are you familiar with any other stories of Christian martyrs? How do these stories strengthen your faith?
- What is religious faith and how does it relate to knowledge?

CHAPTER 6

Knowledge for the Love of God

In chapter 2, I insisted that knowledge matters because it prompts and supports worship and grounds our formation into Christlikeness. Sacrificing and suppressing knowledge, ignoring the life of the mind, on the flip side, leads to idolatry and deformation. I'd like to round back to this for a moment. If you've tracked with me to this point, you might have noticed that I still haven't answered that vital question that plagued me in 2006, the question I couldn't answer when I first set out to be a philosopher. That question was this: Why does knowledge matter once you're a member of God's family? I didn't know the answer then, but I think I do now. Answering this question is crucial; that answer unlocks what Jesus meant when he said that knowing the truth sets us free.

The answer is simple really: extending our knowledge *about* God is essential for deepening our knowledge *of* God. The gospel, in the end, is an offer of relationship with God, of acquaintance with him. In the gospel, we are offered the chance to be with God forever, to be present and laid bare before him without any shame, to experience the abundant life that comes with intimacy with him. We are beckoned back to Eden, where God dwells. As we've seen, knowledge about a thing is not the same as acquaintance with it. I know about Abraham Lincoln, but I don't know *him*. But I want to show you that you can't be acquainted with God without knowledge about him. Here again, the reason is simple: knowledge about God leads to worship and formation, and worship and formation facilitate intimacy with God. On the flip side, idolatry and deformation facilitate relational distance.

~*~

Vitally, this is what the Bible teaches. Consider first the idea that knowledge prompts worship and thereby deepens our knowledge of God. Here is Psalm 100:

> Shout for joy to the LORD, all the earth.
> Worship the LORD with gladness;
> come before him with joyful songs.
> Know that the LORD is God.
> It is he who made us, and we are his;
> we are his people, the sheep of his pasture.
> Enter his gates with thanksgiving and his courts
> with praise;
> give thanks to him and praise his name.
> For the LORD is good and his love endures forever;
> his faithfulness continues through all generations.

The psalmist calls us to acts of praise because of what we know about the Lord. We shout for joy, we worship with gladness, we enter his gates with thanksgiving because we *know that* he is God and *that* he is good and loving and faithful. The Psalms are full of this sort of thing, as is the rest of the Old Testament. Indeed, a central charge against the nation of Israel is that they forget what God has done, and that this leads them into wickedness and idolatry. That is, they forget and so they fail to live the lives that God desires for them.

A similar message abounds in the New Testament. Take Paul's letter to the Romans. In chapter 1, Paul is beginning to develop his argument that all people stand condemned before God, starting with Gentiles (that is, non-Jews). Paul explains,

> For although they knew God, they neither glorified him as God nor gave thanks to him, but their thinking became futile and their foolish hearts were darkened. Although they claimed to be wise, they became fools and exchanged the glory of the immortal God for images. . . . They exchanged the truth about God for a lie, and worshiped and served created things rather than the Creator. (1:21–23, 25)

Here we see that suppressing knowledge, or sacrificing knowledge as I'm putting it, leads to all manner of evil. The evil starts with a failure to worship God and leads inevitably to vicious character and behavior. But Paul doesn't stop there. He does not leave us in despair. He shows the way to redemption, which is of course fundamentally through Jesus. Paul makes clear that part of the recovery—indeed, a central facet of the recovery—proceeds by way of our minds. Later in Romans, Paul says,

> Therefore, I urge you, brothers and sisters, in view of God's mercy, to offer your bodies as a living sacrifice, holy and pleasing to God—this is your true and proper worship. Do not conform to the pattern of this world, but be transformed by the renewing of your mind. Then you will be able to test and approve what God's will is—his good, pleasing and perfect will. (12:1–2)

Notice the progression Paul reveals here. Offer yourselves to God! How? Renew your mind! That way you'll know God's will. Renewal is a matter of the heart, and it starts with the mind, with knowledge of God and his will. With knowledge of who Jesus is and what he has done for us.

Paul isn't alone in this view. These ideas are a refrain of the New Testament. As with the Old Testament, the New Testament speaks with one voice about this: knowledge matters, and it matters because it prompts worship and leads to formation.

~❦~

So knowledge prompts worship and leads to formation. That much is clear. There seems to be another step, though, the step from worship to communion. To take that step, we need to think about what worship is. In Book 10 of *The City of God*, Augustine says,

> To [God] we owe that . . . service, both in ourselves and sacrifices, for we are all His temple, and each one His temple. . . . Our hearts elevated to Him are His altars. His only Son is the Priest by whom we please Him. . . . The gifts He giveth us, we do in vows return to Him. . . . We offer Him the sacrifices of humility and praises on the altar of our heart in the fire of fervent love. . . . He is our blessed founder, and our desires' accomplishment. . . . For our good . . . is nothing but to adhere unto Him. . . . To this good we ought to be led by those that love us, and to lead those we love. . . . So then the command of loving his neighbour, being given to him that knows how to love himself, what does it command but to commend the love of God unto him? This is God's true worship, true piety, true religion, and due service to God only.[1]

Worship, in other words, involves entering the presence of God with the posture appropriate to being in God's presence. We adore, confess, praise, repent, sing, tremble, and give thanks because we see who God is and, in and by relation to him, who we are as well. We recognize our dependence and need in the light of God's presence, and this is what leads us to bow down, to offer ourselves as a sacrifice. In that self-sacrifice, we are led to Christlikeness in one way, while being reminded of our need for Christ in another. We are like Jesus in that we sacrifice ourselves for our God. But, unlike Jesus, we are not forsaken in the midst of our sacrifice. We are instead welcomed into God's presence because of Jesus's sacrifice for us.

Theologians Duncan Forrester, Ian McDonald, and Gian Tellini endorse Augustine's vision of worship. "In worship," they say, "God is encountered and glorified, God's purposes are discerned, however faintly, and God's people are nourished and strengthened for service. . . . In worship we are in touch with the life of heaven."[2] They even call their book introducing Christian worship *Encounter with God*. Worship *just is* encountering God. To worship is to enter God's presence, and it is there that we receive life. This is just what Augustine argued for centuries earlier. And it's what the psalmist describes in Psalm 100. We enter God's courts through his gates and so we come before him. Worship is presence with God. This is the Christian view, ancient and modern.

Here's the point: worship leads us into communion with God because, ultimately, worship *is* communion with God. The step from worship to communion is then as short as a step can be. That knowledge leads us to worship means that knowledge leads us into communion with God. Paul's command to offer yourself as a living sacrifice is a command to worship, which is a command to commune with God. And so Paul is saying that the renewal of our minds through the acquisition of knowledge about God in the end moves us toward knowledge of God.

～❦

Well, that's what the Bible and the Christian tradition *say*. But is it *true*? In chapter 8, I hope to convince you that we can know even if all we have is the Bible. In this present case, happily, we've got both the Bible and other sources!

It turns out to be rather obvious, when you reflect on the connection between propositional knowledge (knowledge *that* such-and-such, or reasonable true belief) and knowledge by acquaintance (knowledge *of*, or intimacy with, something or someone), that this is what you should expect for our relationship with God. To see this, I want to consider a different sort of relationship: the relationship my children have with one another. From the day Gretchen was born, it's been a precious thing to watch the pair of them together. For many years, and I hope it's forever, Lyle has thought of Gretchen as his best friend, and Gretchen has thought of Lyle as hers. They both, at different times and before they really understood the idea of marriage, would say they wanted to marry one another. Now that thought would horrify them! But at the time, this thought of marriage they shared was, of course, just a childlike expression of relational intimacy. A glorious thing, really.

So think about that relationship. They both know each other, and in that *acquaintance* way we all want and hope to know God. And now imagine that a group of strangers, maybe new classmates on his first day of college, ask Lyle about Gretchen. They have never met her, but they ask because they desire to approximate the knowledge by acquaintance that Lyle certainly possesses and that they realize they lack. Imagine Lyle gives this reply: "Well, sure, I *know* Gretchen. I've been acquainted with her for her whole life! But, I mean, what makes you think that means I know anything *about* her?" That would be a strange speech. It borders on incoherent, in fact. To say that you know someone and yet know nothing *about* them is ridiculous. Deepening acquaintance simply *requires* extending propositional knowledge.

This is, of course, not unique to Lyle and Gretchen. It goes for my relationship with Jamie, too. If I knew nothing about her, how could I claim to know her? To know Jamie well, I must minimally be able to physically distinguish her from others. The demands to love her well are far less trivial. I must know her hopes and fears and dreams, what she thinks and longs for, and what she loves and hates. So it goes for our relationships with each of our children, and for our children with their friends, and for their friends with their families and their families' friends, and on and on. No personal relationship is exempt from this connection between knowledge by acquaintance and propositional knowledge.

Our knowledge of God is bound up with our knowledge about him in just the same way. Why would it be any different? *How* could it be any different? And this is why Jesus cares so much about knowledge. The knowledge of himself that frees us to be fully human requires knowledge about him, the gospel, ourselves, and the world God has made.

The Scriptures teach this, too. Take Psalm 27:

> The LORD is my light and my salvation—
>   whom shall I fear?
> The LORD is the stronghold of my life—
>   of whom shall I be afraid? . . .
> One thing I ask from the LORD, this only do I seek:
> that I may dwell in the house of the LORD
>   all the days of my life,
> To gaze on the beauty of the LORD and
>   to seek him in his temple. . . .
> Hear my voice when I call, LORD;
>   be merciful to me and answer me.
> My heart says of you, "Seek his face!"
>   Your face, LORD, I will seek.
> Do not hide your face from me . . .
>   you have been my helper. . . .

I remain confident of this: I will see the goodness of
the LORD in the land of the living.
Wait for the LORD; be strong and take heart
and wait for the LORD.

This is a beautiful meditation on what we all really need as humans: intimacy with our Father in heaven. Implicitly, we can see how knowledge about God relates to knowledge *of* God. But you also see the psalmist, in his passion to dwell in God's house, speaking with clarity and confidence about who God is, what he has done, where he is to be found, and what he will do in the future. Think of it this way: the psalmist knows whom he seeks, he is able to identify the house where he desires to dwell, and he knows why that house is a good place to be. It's not just any house the psalmist desires, it's God's house. And it's God's house the psalmist desires because God is the one who saves.

When you don't know *about* God, you don't know where to look for him, and you don't know why you should look for him in the first place. And if you don't know those things, you won't be able to find him even if you wanted, and you won't be motivated to find him anyway. Yet, all this knowledge about him isn't enough. We need more, but we can't get the more that we need—knowledge *of* him—without knowledge about him. We need more, not less. Propositional knowledge, in other words, supports and enhances knowledge by acquaintance.

⁓⊕⁓

This connection between propositional knowledge and knowledge by acquaintance is the piece of the puzzle that was missing for me in 2006. At root, what I needed was a way to order my intellectual life around something that mattered to the mundane realities of my life in graduate school. That knowledge about God supports and enhances knowledge of God is a crucial insight. It would have given me a vital tool to find meaning in my day-to-day existence as a philosophy graduate student. It would not have been difficult for me to see the way my studies were ways of studying God and his creation. And that would have been enough, at least insofar as my troubles were intellectual, to help me find meaning in my studies beyond its capacity to land me a job as an academic. It would have given me confidence, as it has now, that by learning about God and his world, I am gaining tools for drawing near to God. Knowledge takes us deeper into the Triune life of our God in heaven.

There is one final step on the path from propositional knowledge to love, and it's the step from acquaintance to love. Acquaintance with God, with God's Triune life, is acquaintance with the *love* of God. The love of God, *the* characteristic of God's life, is something knowledge helps us experience. And so knowledge is, in this sense, for the love of God. Knowledge is for the love of God in a different sense as well. We love—whether our love is of God or our neighbor—because God first loved us (1 John 4:19). Knowledge, then, takes us to God, where we experience God's love, and that experience of divine love allows us to love in return. Our love for God and our neighbor, therefore, is enabled and supported by the knowledge that deepens our acquaintance with God. Knowledge about God begets acquaintance with God, which begets experience of divine love, which begets love of God and our neighbor. Knowledge is, in this dual sense, *for the love of God.*

What I wanted was a reason to pursue philosophical knowledge, and we've found one. Knowledge is for the love of God. This fact supplies a reason for us to pursue knowledge in any area, philosophy included. This is true whether or not there is a clear or obvious connection between what we learn and great theological truths. All of creation is God's handiwork, and so even the smallest, most seemingly meaningless facts are testaments to his creativity, intelligence, and providential care. All knowledge—and I mean *all*—is for the love of God.

—❧—

I have a confession. I'm holding back. There is even more to this story.

Chapter 6 Discussion Questions

- Think of a time when learning or experiencing something new prompted you to worship God. Have you had a similar experience that didn't prompt you to worship? What was different about you or the situation in the two cases?
- How can we be confident that we are in the presence of God?
- Reflect on Romans 1. Do you see signs of worship of the creation in your own heart? Are there truths you are suppressing?
- How can we seek to know God? What practical ways can we grow in our knowledge of our Lord?
- Are you actively seeking to know God more, or have you become complacent in that regard? What is encouraging you to pursue God, or conversely, what is holding you back?
- Why does God ask us to love him with our mind? What is knowledge for?

Part Three

Complications

CHAPTER 7

Can We Know Things Apart from Science?

D espite being a philosopher now, I started my life headed in
the direction of math and science. In fact, this continued
more or less all the way through my career as an undergraduate at
the University of North Texas. I wound up getting my bachelor's
degree in economics with a minor in mathematics. I came very
close to traipsing off to the University of Michigan, where I had
been admitted to the doctoral program in economics, but wound
up turning to philosophy just before I graduated. I first moved onto
the campus of UNT as a high schooler, believe it or not. I spent
my junior and senior years living in McConnell Hall, a dorm that
houses around 400 high schoolers who compose the student body
of the Texas Academy of Mathematics and Science (TAMS). This is
where I earned my high school diploma. As a TAMS student, I took
classes with ordinary college students, emphasizing sciences like biology, chemistry, and physics and various branches of mathematics,
mostly calculus and its cousins.

My time at TAMS was undeniably formative. In part, that's
because I made lifelong friendships, including with folks who
have done amazing things in the world. I can say honestly that my
high school classmates are among the most gifted people I've ever

known. So many of them went on to become doctors or lawyers, or to earn PhDs in everything from engineering to psychology to theology. More importantly, TAMS is where I started following Jesus. But that's a story for another time.

I bring up TAMS in large measure to say this: I love math and science. I have views of which numbers are the best. (Easy cases: primes are better than non-primes, and twin primes are better than other primes.) I see the world in a very mathematical way. And I've spent a lot of time studying various branches of science, from physics to psychology. My life has been informed and enriched by that inquiry, and it's undeniable that science has in many ways made the world a better place. I would be so very proud if either or both of my children became scientists.

~❀~

Not all Christians share my view about this. And many non-Christians would think that a science-loving Christian is something of an oxymoron. Given my background in science and mathematics, and as a Christian, I've always found this puzzling. But the idea that science and faith stand in some kind of conflict is simultaneously pernicious and pervasive. I mentioned this in an earlier chapter, so I won't repeat myself here except to say: Christians have always believed in both special *and* general revelation, and that these really are *revelation*, and that Jesus wants us to take both seriously. (This is not to say that science is the only form general revelation takes.) My immediate concern is instead with the idea that science is somehow better than theology, that science is what gives us *knowledge*, whereas theology can only give us (unjustified) belief or (blind) faith.

Take Richard Dawkins. He consistently says things along the following lines: "Perhaps there are some genuinely profound and meaningful questions that are forever beyond the reach of science. . . . But if science cannot answer some ultimate question, what makes anybody think that religions can?"[1] He makes clear his view that theology, if it counts as a discipline with a subject matter at all, does not operate by drawing conclusions from actual evidence.[2] The theologies of the traditional monotheistic religions are "founded on local traditions of private revelation rather than evidence."[3] However Dawkins ought to be interpreted, it's quite clear that he believes theology is intellectually inferior to science. Indeed, the idea that theology is not a field of inquiry that is concerned with evidence suggests, given the connection between evidence and knowledge I've already highlighted, that theology cannot deliver knowledge at all. Science, on the other hand, is at least in principle able to produce knowledge. And of course, if Dawkins is right that theology doesn't deliver knowledge, then it's no surprise that he characterizes faith in the way that he does: "persistent false belief in the face of strong contradictory evidence."[4] You can perhaps guess how I might respond to Dawkins's claims. But I'd rather not go into that at the moment. I just use him as an example of the sort of trend I'm highlighting, to give assurances that I'm not just making up problems where there really are none.

There are more subtle, and so more troubling, expressions of this sort of thing. In February 2006, just after my graduate school crisis began, *National Geographic* published an essay by Lauren Slater called "True Love." Near the beginning of the article, Slater says this: "We have relied on stories to explain the complexities of love, tales of jealous gods and arrows. Now, however, these stories— so much a part of every civilization—may be changing as science steps in to explain what we have always felt to be myth, to be magic. For the first time, new research has begun to illuminate where love lies in the brain, the particulars of its chemical components."[5]

It's that last bit that really got me. Slater is suggesting that scientists are beginning to explain the chemical components of love.

Not the chemical components of the physical correlates of love. The chemical components of *love itself*. This expresses a particular view about the relationship between mental states like love and belief and pain on the one hand, and physical states like goings-on in your brain on the other. It's a view philosophers call *physicalism*, the idea that (roughly) minds are identical to brains, that mental states *just are* brain states. I think that view is false, but not crazy. What's striking about Slater's claim is not that, though. What's striking is that the question whether that view is true or false *doesn't even arise*. She simply assumes that science can tell us everything we could know about love. Implicit in Slater's article is, then, the idea that any source apart from science, like theology or philosophy, must consist in appeals to myth or magic.

What in the world happened? How did we get to the point that these ideas could be taken seriously, much less that they would be thought of as mandatory? Even more importantly, what should we say about Dawkins's ideas, and Slater's?

─✲─

The story of the genesis of these ideas is fascinating. It begins in earnest around the time of the Scientific Revolution of the mid-sixteenth century, the same period I mentioned in chapter 3 as the beginning of the modernist notion of truth. This was a period of great intellectual upheaval, and much of the controversy had to do with understanding the relationship between faith and reason. One aspect of that understanding concerns what to think when the deliverances of science conflict with the deliverances of theology. A new conception of physical science had emerged, a conception more or less identical to how our culture naturally thinks of science today. One striking difference between this conception and the older, medieval conception had to do with whether science was subject to the authority of philosophy and theology. Ancient and medieval Christian thinkers maintained that general revelation in all its forms, including physical science, was subject to correction by special revelation. Modern scientists were having none of this. Where questions about the physical world were concerned, science was king.

This is not to say that early modern thinkers rejected the authority of Scripture. Far from it, actually. But they had a revolutionary view of science that gave it authority over even Scripture in the physical domain. Scripture and science both had authority, but each in their own domain. Galileo Galilei, the great sixteenth-to seventeenth-century Italian scientist, was an exemplar of this compromise. Here is an excerpt from a letter Galileo wrote to the Grand Duchess Christina in 1615:

> I think that in discussions of physical problems we ought to begin not from the authority of scriptural passages, but from sense-experiences and necessary demonstrations; for the holy Bible and the phenomena of nature proceed alike from the divine Word, the former as the dictate of the Holy Ghost and the latter as the observant executrix of God's commands. It is necessary for the Bible, in order to be accommodated to the understanding of every man, to speak many things which appear to differ from the absolute truth so far as the bare meaning of the words is concerned. But Nature, on the other hand, is inexorable and immutable; she never transgresses the laws imposed upon her, or cares a whit whether her abstruse reasons and methods of operation are understandable to men. For that reason it appears that nothing physical which sense-experience sets before our eyes, or which necessary demonstrations prove to us, ought to be called in question (much less condemned) upon the testimony of biblical passages which may have some different meaning beneath their words.[6]

Part of what is striking here is that you see Galileo wrestling with giving science its due without compromising the authority of the Bible. He rightly recognizes the supremacy of Christ in supplying both general and special revelation. Indeed, this is why he is so confident in the deliverances of science! But notice that he marginalizes the Bible when it comes to the physical world: "Nothing physical which sense-experience sets before our eyes . . . ought to be called in question . . . upon the testimony of biblical passages." That's the mistake he makes. This is the first step along the way to Dawkins and Slater.

The rest of the journey is, to be honest, fairly complicated. But the short version goes something like this. Galileo's (and others') view that theology should not compete with science when it comes to the physical world caught hold of the imagination of not only scientists but philosophers and even the general public. And science was giving us profound new insights into the workings of the world. Or anyway, the purported insights of science were helping unlock technological advancements, advancements that promised a better life for all humanity. It was, therefore, increasingly difficult to challenge the credentials of science. In the meantime, to retain a proper domain for theology, thinkers divided the world into the physical and the nonphysical. Science, the thought went, could have the physical domain. Theology (and such) got the nonphysical. (Thinkers prior to the Scientific Revolution would have accepted the distinction between the physical and the nonphysical, but they would not have thought it so sharp or so fundamental a divide.) When this division of labor was enacted, there was much that science could not explain, much that seemed to fall under the auspices of theology, much that was attributed to the workings of the nonphysical (including God). But slowly science claimed more and more of the world as its own. Less and less remained for theology, more and more explanations in terms of the nonphysical gave way to explanations in terms of the physical.

The chief hurdle along this path was humanity itself. Humanity, it seemed, could not be fully explained in purely physical, scientific terms. God, it seemed, was needed to explain the origins of humanity. And nonphysical souls, it seemed, were needed to explain the complexity of human nature and culture. Then along came Charles Darwin. Darwin's theory of the origin of the variety and complexity of living things on planet earth, deploying centrally the idea of common descent through absolutely unguided—that is, random—variations, unhooked the modern, rational mind from its need for a Creator. Just a generation later, Nietzsche declared the death of God.

That is—I hope rather obviously—a simplification of the historical record, as most of my historical musings have been in this book. But it gives you a real sense of the highlights of the story, of the central, dominant features of the subject.

⁓❦⁓

There's another thing I should mention about science. Science, as it developed from Galileo onward, increasingly moved from a concern to describe the literal truth of the physical world toward a concern to develop mathematically precise models that make accurate predictions. Scientists wanted, in other words, to be able to explain what will come next, given a description of what came before. Whether these descriptions were actually, literally *true* took a back seat. What was really important was whether a scientific theory *worked*, whether it served its technological purpose. "Truth," in the context of the most fundamental areas of science, is not really about correspondence to reality. The underlying conception of truth in the world of science is *instrumentalist*. What I mean is that science is first concerned with making predictions. Good scientific theories are merely tools—*instruments*—for making sense of what we observe and predicting what we'll observe in the future.

Whether the claims of a theory match the real world is of, at best, secondary importance.

Now, this probably comes as a surprise. The standard story we're told about science is that it is concerned to describe the objective facts of reality. No doubt that is a concern of many scientists, and no doubt they do that quite well. However, the underlying methodology of the theoretical branches of science (theoretical physics, most notably, but also the most abstract branches of chemistry and biology) is to construct models of reality in order to make more and more accurate predictions. (Less theoretical branches of science, like various areas of engineering, zoology, etc., are a different, more complicated story.) Whether those models correspond to reality is less relevant. What really matters is whether scientific models are instrumentally "true."

I'd like to assure you I'm not just making all this up. Mitch Stokes wrote a fascinating book called *How to Be an Atheist*. It's a weird title because Stokes is a Christian! The upshot of the book is that we need to be more cognizant of what science is really all about so that we can take it more seriously. The surprise, according to Stokes, is that when you take science super-seriously, you're led to be much more skeptical of scientific claims, at least if you understand science as concerned with truth. Stokes documents, in rather alarming detail, actual scientists and secular philosophers of science who endorse the idea that science should be conceived in an instrumentalist way.

Here is a characteristic example. Stokes notes that Arthur Fine, a world-class philosopher of science, asserts that these days, "Most [scientists] who actually use [general relativity] think of the theory as a powerful instrument, rather than as expressing a 'big truth.'"[7] And commenting on Werner Heisenberg's pioneering work on quantum mechanics, Fine says, "Heisenberg's seminal paper of 1925 is prefaced by the following abstract, announcing, in effect, his philosophical stance: 'In this paper an attempt will be made to obtain bases for a quantum-theoretical mechanics based exclusively on relations between quantities observable in principle.' In the body of the paper, Heisenberg not only rejects any reference to unobservables, he also moves away from the very idea that one should try to form any picture of a reality underlying his mechanics."[8]

In other words, Heisenberg was unconcerned with describing reality. What he wanted was to make predictions. There are many, many more passages like this in the Stokes book, and they involve everyone from Einstein to Heisenberg to Bohr, and more besides. Modern science, especially the hard sciences, is rooted in an instrumentalist conception of science. Science is there to make predictions, not fundamentally to describe reality.

I want to be clear about something. I'm not criticizing science for this! It is, absolutely, a valid and useful task to produce models that allow us to make predictions about what will follow from particular circumstances. When engineering an airplane, for example, one needn't worry whether gravity is produced by massive bodies curving spacetime or by the exchange of particles. All that matters is whether the gravitational force of the earth on that giant tube of metal we call an "airplane" can be overcome by the pressure differential between the air on the top and bottom of the wings. Making predictions is a vital, absolutely valid goal of scientific study.

So I point all this out not to criticize science, but to make a simple point: scientific methodology doesn't exist in a vacuum. That methodology makes assumptions, and those assumptions ought to be put to the test, like the assumptions of any other discipline. Further, those assumptions place natural boundaries around the aspects of reality that science can study. And I don't mean just the physical world as opposed to the nonphysical. I mean something much deeper than that. I mean that we ought to be open to the possibility that science *has significant limits that the very nature of science prevents it from overcoming.* And this means that there might even be questions about physical reality that science simply cannot handle, despite its magnificence.

Here's a simple example, one that I think even scientists can accept. Science is in the business of learning things on the basis of the way that bits of the world modify other bits of the world. So, for example, chemists work very hard to understand how different chemicals interact, and construct theories—models!—of chemical composition in order to help us understand why those reactions occur. And all of this takes place by making empirical observations about particular interactions and endeavoring to organize them into simple, coherent, powerful theories. This is not true just in chemistry; it's true in all areas of science. And it's great! One result of these scientific endeavors, however, has been a cosmological theory according to which there are aspects of physical reality that are forever beyond the reach of empirical observation (because they are outside our "light cone"). Given where we exist in time and space, we simply cannot, in principle, accumulate any evidence about the goings-on in these parts of the universe.

The point is just that the methodology of science requires that it proceed by making empirical observations, and there are things that simply leave no detectable empirical traces. Sometimes the reason no empirical traces are detectable is because the things are just too far away in time and space. But sometimes the reason is more principled, is deeper in the fabric of reality. Science simply cannot explain the existence of the scientific laws they've worked so diligently and ingeniously to uncover. Still more radically, at the bottom of the physical world, wherever that bottom is, scientists cannot gain insights into the basic nature of causal interactions among those fundamental physical bits. What I mean is that, at the fundamental level, science can at best describe a cause and its effect; it simply cannot describe *why* this-here fundamental cause produces that-there fundamental effect. Appeals to laws of nature won't do. The law of gravity itself isn't what makes bodies with mass exert a gravitational force on one another. Laws aren't themselves causes. They simply describe patterns of cause and effect that are stable across the known universe. As John Lennox, an emeritus professor of mathematics at Oxford, puts it, "the laws of nature *describe* the universe, but they actually *explain* nothing."[9]

Therefore, there are questions even about the natural world— good questions, valid questions—that science cannot answer. I see no reason to think that requires us to think that we can't know the answer to those questions. All it means is that we'd better have some other avenue to gain knowledge of the natural world.

~

I mentioned my friend J. P. Moreland in chapter 4. He's a philosopher, too, and works with me at Biola. Maybe it's better to say I work with him. He was my teacher long before we became colleagues. My first academic publication was coauthored with J. P., and it emerged from a term paper I wrote for a course he taught. I already described our chance encounter in Oxford. Needless to say, I've great affection, admiration, and appreciation for J. P. (I didn't intend that alliteration!) Anyway, like I did, J. P. started out in the world of science and turned to philosophy rather late. His undergraduate education was in chemistry, and he has always loved science. J. P. has worked extensively on questions about the nature and limits of science. He's read, thought, and written about these issues *a lot*.

In 2018, J. P. published a book called *Scientism and Secularism.* I'm concerned mostly with the *scientism* bit of that title duo. *Scientism* is the view of science that I've been fussing about, the view we find explicitly in Dawkins and implicitly in Slater. It's the view that science is the only path to knowledge, or at least that it's way better than any other path.

One of the prongs of J. P.'s argument against scientism is really rather simple: he points out that we obviously know certain truths without having any scientific evidence whatever for them.[10] For example, you know that $2 + 2 = 4$, that all squares are rectangles, and as we all do that the first derivative of the sine function is the cosine function. (Yes, everyone should learn calculus.) You also know that nothing can be both true and false at the same time. These are just a few examples of mathematical and logical truths that everyone knows by rational insight, not by science. You also know your own mind, your conscious states, without the aid of science. You use introspection—that amazing capacity we have to "look inside," as it were—to know that your head hurts, or that you believe that God exists, or that all us Potterheads are afraid of dementors. All these were things humans knew long before we began investigating the world scientifically. (Well, maybe not the one about dementors.) Finally, you know that kicking puppies is cruel, that murdering infants is morally reprehensible, and that generosity toward the poor and marginalized is good. We know these moral truths without science, too. Indeed, not only does science not teach us these truths—whether logical, mathematical, moral, or about our own minds—science in principle is incapable of delivering knowledge of these truths. They are just not scientifically knowable.

There are complications. Because of course there are. Let me mention just two. First, it's true that advances in neuroscience are allowing us to understand how states of consciousness relate to states of our central nervous system. In this way, we may someday get to a point where we can know whether someone is in a particular conscious state using scientific tools. And you might think that this means that science alone can give us knowledge of our conscious states. But this is misleading, and for a simple reason: neuroscientists can't establish the correlations without asking people what's going on in their minds! The correlations between conscious states and brain states can only be known via the aid of introspective awareness. Science alone is simply not enough.

Second complication. There have been influential attempts to explain morality in more scientifically acceptable terms. Hedonism, for example, attempts to describe morality ultimately in terms of pain and pleasure, that is, in terms of things that are more empirically detectable than old categories like virtue and obligation. There are nonhedonistic theories attempting something similar. It's no surprise, given the story about modernism that I told you earlier, that these theories arose not long after Galileo. And theories like hedonism have been influential. In many ways, the public morality of our time is more or less a kind of hedonism. At any rate, these theories may look rather scientific, but they nonetheless are not acceptable in general, nor by the lights of scientism. For one thing, they just have serious problems getting the moral facts right. Sacrifice on behalf of others is often painful, but it is nevertheless very, very good. For another, pain and pleasure are conscious states, and so specific moral facts won't be knowable by purely scientific means. For a third thing, the central claim of these sorts of views— that pain is bad, for example—is not scientifically verifiable. No amount of science will bridge the chasm from pain to badness.

Importantly, these complications don't alter the point: moral knowledge and knowledge of our own minds is beyond the reach of science alone, but these are, without a doubt, domains of knowledge. We know certain moral truths and certain parts of our own minds.

~❦~

The upshot of all this is really quite clear: you can know things apart from science. In fact, many of the most important bits of knowledge that I and others have—that taking innocent life is unfailingly wrong, that loving your neighbor is unfailingly good, that I love my children with everything I am, that I continue to exist despite profound changes through the years in my body and in my psychology—are truths for which scientific evidence is either flimsy or nonexistent. Nevertheless we know these things with borderline certainty. Furthermore, vast swaths of what we know are truths backed by solid scientific evidence *that we as individuals simply do not have.* I've never done a single empirical psychological study, much less operated the Large Hadron Collider, and yet I take myself to know what certain psychological studies and physical experiments have revealed about God's good world.

Once again, don't hear what I'm not saying. It's okay that we didn't collect the direct scientific evidence! In large part, it's okay because we have other kinds of evidence, like the testimony of experts, that assures us of the truths we believe. Testimony is a crucial source of knowledge, an important source, a source that is both good and necessary to get along in the world.

We can, in other words, know things, even desperately important things, without the direct aid of science and sometimes without science at all, even in principle. Science is great! But it's not the only path to knowledge. Not because science is bad or problematic or something, but just because it has *limits.*

I'm planning to return to this idea of testimony in the next chapter. In a way, understanding this point about how science shaped my experience during my doctoral program requires understanding a different issue, an issue connected intimately to trusting the Scriptures.

Chapter 7 Discussion Questions

- How would you describe science to someone who had never heard of it? What is the picture of science you implicitly operate with?
- What are some of the limits of scientific knowledge? Were you surprised/challenged by the claims in this chapter about the nature and limits of science?
- It seems as if some people abandon Christianity when they learn about the world through science. Why do you think that is? What mistakes do people make when they think that science disproves Christianity?
- Can science reveal anything about God?
- What are two examples of important things you know without the aid of science? Be concrete and specific!

CHAPTER 8

Can We Know Something Simply Because the Bible Says It's So?

I've been thinking a lot about how hard it can be to stay faithful to God these days. I found faithfulness difficult during my time as a graduate student. And I've been thinking of that as a way to look for clues about how to teach my own children and my students a better way. As I've mentioned before, I want so badly for them to follow Jesus. It's the reason I'm writing this book. Staying faithful is hard for two interrelated reasons. The first is that the world is a mess. There's so much pain and sorrow. No doubt this is or will be true for each of us individually, but also for those we love. This has always been true, and it's always made faithfulness difficult.

When my children were young, Jamie read them a number of the books in the *Chronicles of Narnia*. We even listened to *Prince Caspian* and *The Horse and His Boy* on road trips to Seattle or Texas, or maybe both. (Jamie would know.) The author of these stories, C. S. Lewis, was a fascinating man. He wrote lots of other books too, many of which have had a significant impact on Jamie and me. Just recently I read one of Lewis's books for the first time. It's called *A Grief Observed*. It's a kind of memoir in which Lewis wrestles with the death of his beloved wife, Joy. In the opening pages, after describing the way grief feels sometimes like fear, sometimes like drunkenness, the coming and going of "tears and pathos," and the "laziness of grief," Lewis says this:

> Meanwhile, where is God? This is one of the most disquieting symptoms. When you are happy, so happy that you have no sense of needing Him, so happy that you are tempted to feel His claims upon you as an interruption, if you remember yourself and turn to Him with gratitude and praise, you will be—or so it feels—welcomed with open arms. But go to Him when your need is desperate, when all other help is vain, and what do you find? A door slammed in your face, and a sound of bolting and double bolting on the inside. After that, silence. You may as well turn away. The longer you wait, the more emphatic the silence will become. There are no lights in the windows. It might be an empty house. Was it ever inhabited? It seemed so once. And that seeming was as strong as this. What can this mean? Why is He so present a commander in our time of prosperity and so very absent a help in time of trouble?[1]

If that's not wrenching enough, Lewis goes on: "The real danger is of coming to believe such dreadful things about [God]. The conclusion I dread is not 'So there's no God after all,' but 'So this is what God's really like. Deceive yourself no longer.'"[2] The world is evil. And that challenges belief in a good God.

What do you do with this sort of suffering and grief? I think we must—*I* must—like the psalmists so consistently do, take it to God in brutally honest prayer. Jesus, after all, knows what it's like to feel betrayed by the Father. "Why have you forsaken me?" he cried from the cross. But because Jesus is God incarnate, his connection with the Father could not be more intimate. Interesting that even Jesus had feelings that didn't match the reality of his connection to the Father. I find this comforting.

This chapter isn't supposed to be about evil or about God's hiddenness in the midst of suffering. I bring up Lewis because his witness shows a path toward faithfulness even in the midst of suffering, if you get right the issue this chapter is really about: knowing through the Bible. We must talk and read and think about evil and hiddenness, but as the bride of Christ and with attention on him, ordered by what God has to say in the Bible. I'll return to these ideas.

~&

I said there were two reasons why faithfulness to Christ is so hard, but so far have gotten only to one of them. The second reason exacerbates the first and blunts the Christian's most compelling retort to suffering and evil. The second reason is that we are taught so incessantly to believe that religion is a private matter that's just between you and God, or is perhaps just inside you if God is merely a human fabrication. But as we've seen, Christianity in the first instance makes claims about how reality really is and therefore connects our hope in Christ to real events in history. In the second instance it makes demands on how you live your real life, day in and day out.

One manifestation of the cultural insistence on the privacy of religion and faith is the elevation of science, which we covered in the last chapter. But another manifestation is the flip side of that scientistic coin: a devaluing of the Bible. It used to be that the Scriptures, interpreted and clarified by the church, were the Christian's most important source of knowledge. That's not to say that we don't use the evidence of our senses and our innate moral faculty and our ability to reason just as much as, and probably more than, the Scriptures. But if you think about our high-level beliefs about the basic makeup of the world, the nature of God and ourselves, the grand story of reality, and the foundation and central pillars of morality and the good life, then I think it's right that Christians used to look to the Scriptures first and foremost. Returning to the last chapter momentarily, if we can't know anything apart from science about these important things, then the Scriptures alone can't give you knowledge of them.

Embracing the idea that the Scriptures don't supply us with knowledge is the death of a person's devotion to the Father, Son, and Holy Spirit. The Scriptures, as theologians put it, have authority and primacy in the life of the Christian. Biblical authority means that we must follow the teachings of the Bible. Biblical primacy means that we must look first and foremost to the Bible on those high-level matters about the basic makeup of the world, the nature of God and ourselves, the grand story of reality, and the foundation and central pillars of morality and the good life.

The reason believing the Scriptures supply us with knowledge matters so much for devotion to God is because there are vitally important truths on the pages of the Bible, truths that aren't available from other sources. Some of these truths are relevant to bearing up under pain and sorrow and suffering. The apostle Paul, for example, says to the church in Rome, and to us, that "in all things God works for the good of those who love him" (Rom. 8:28). Well, that sounds more or less ridiculous, and it certainly doesn't seem to be the way the world works, given only my powers of observation and rational reflection. It's also something Paul saw fit to say to the Romans in his discussion of suffering. Indeed, Paul's reminder is so vital precisely because our eyes just don't—maybe they *can't*—see suffering work for good.

Now, there's a lot to say about the Bible as a source of knowledge. There's lots of good stuff out there about the historical reliability of the Gospels and the New Testament, about the troubles you might have with how God acts in the Old Testament, about seeming inconsistencies, about tension with contemporary science, and on and on. I don't want to talk about any of that. In part, that's because other people have said it better than I ever could.[3] But in part it's because I want to focus on something else.

I want to assume that God is, in some sense or other, the Author of Scripture. (There's a lot to say about this, too!) This is something C. S. Lewis believed, along with the whole of the church from its inception. An important truth follows immediately from this starting point: the Scriptures are a mode of divine speech. Augustine talked about them as letters from our heavenly home.[4] That is, God speaks to us through the Scriptures. Therefore, we ought to attend carefully to what the Scriptures teach and endeavor to believe the things we discern in the words of the Bible. The Bible is God's testimony to us, his beloved children.

C. S. Lewis lost Joy on July 13, 1960. Roughly seven years earlier, on August 3, 1953, Lewis penned a letter to one Emily McLay. In the letter, Lewis wrestles with tensions he sees in the text of Scripture between divine providence and human freedom, especially as it relates to our salvation. What's striking is that Lewis doesn't go very far toward resolving the tension and seems perfectly comfortable with not being able to chart a resolution. He says very explicitly, in the first sentence of the letter, why he can remain confident about the issues that give rise to the tension even without a clear resolution: "I take it as a first principle that we must not interpret any one part of Scripture so that it contradicts other parts."[5] Lewis seems to draw this principle from a more general commitment to the idea that Scripture, rightly interpreted, can't contradict knowledge derived from any source whatever. Where there seems to be a contradiction, something has gone wrong either with our interpretation of Scripture or our understanding of the book of nature, or both. (Galileo was so close!) One suspects that these sorts of settled commitments, this sort of knowledge, stabilized Lewis while he grieved the loss of Joy. It does not erase the grief. But it must have helped

Lewis, faced with what seemed to be God's darkened house in 1960, to follow his own advice to McLay: "One must NOT . . . believe, on the strength of Scripture or on any other evidence, that God is in any way evil."[6]

Is it acceptable to read the Bible in this way? In a word: yes. If we assume, as I am assuming here, that God wrote the Bible, then in fact we have no choice.

~✦

Is this chapter over so soon? We've already answered its central question! As Christians, *of course* we believe that we can know things if God tells us, and we believe that God is the Author of Scripture, and so *of course* we can know something just because the Bible says it's so.

No, the chapter isn't over. There are pervasive even if unrecognized worries that this picture of the Bible is unworkable. I want to persuade you that it's not crazy to read the Bible like Lewis, to believe that a loving, personal, all-knowing God is speaking to us in its pages, and that this must constrain how we interpret its words. The first step is a quick examination of one root of the unease we feel about this posture toward the Bible.

~✦

A brief opening gambit.

One thing about our scientistic culture that sometimes goes unnoticed is that, by virtue of devaluing the importance of tradition and testimony, it subtly but unfailingly encourages us to privatize our religious beliefs. To privatize a belief is to think of it as something that relates only to ourselves, as if we have made it up or as if its content doesn't answer to the world outside of us. Remember that modern-postmodern combo platter we considered in chapter 3? We're back to that again.

This combo platter shapes our reading of Scripture. In particular, we read the Bible as if it weren't *really* making claims about the
world. As we've seen, Christianity will not abide that idea. Christianity is a religion rooted in history, in the death and resurrection
of Jesus Christ. One cannot privatize these realities.

⁓❧

Let's talk about testimony a bit, since that's what I'm saying the
Bible is. Giving and receiving testimony is an utterly mundane fact
about the human experience. It's so mundane, in fact, that it's easy
to overlook. An astoundingly large segment of our knowledge is
derived exclusively from the testimony of others. And some of this
knowledge constitutes the heart of our self-conception and of the
way we navigate reality.

I have this friend named Josh. He's one of the smartest people
I've ever known, has a PhD in philosophy from one of the top two
or three doctoral programs in the world. Josh grew up in Southern
California with a younger brother. They were separated by almost
exactly two years in age, birthdays just days apart. Despite that
Josh's birthday was April 24 and his brother's was April 27, they
always celebrated together, with a single party. When Josh was close
to turning sixteen, he needed his birth certificate to get his driver's
license. His parents, after some rummaging, produced one for him.
Josh studied it, and to his surprise and dismay discovered that the
birth certificate reported that his birthday was April 27! His parents,
it seemed, had confused Josh's and his brother's respective birthdays. Josh had grown up mistaken about the day he was born.

Why is this so weird? (Josh describes it in more traumatic
terms . . .) It's so weird because the primary evidence we have about
our birthday is *testimonial*. It's the testimony of our parents. And
that testimony is rarely wrong. Indeed, unless you're wildly unlucky
like Josh was, you absolutely *know* your birthday, just on the basis of

your parents' testimony. (I'm leaving aside far more tragic cases of neglect or abuse or loss; describing such cases as simply "unlucky" seems cold-hearted at best.) Notice, by the way, that birth certificates are testimonial, too. A person's birth certificate is testimony from his or her parents, a doctor or nurse or whatever, and maybe some hospital staff. Josh went from relying on one sort of testimony about his birthday to another sort. But the testimony itself is ineliminable for him, as it is for the rest of us.

So much of what we know, we know by testimony. Other than the evidence of our own senses, testimony may be the single most important source of information we have about reality. Testimony is one of the primary ways we know what's going on inside the minds of others. People tell us what they believe, feel, want, and so on. There's no other way to know, especially with any specificity. Even using body language for this type of knowledge is derivative, since we've learned to read body language by pairing what people's bodies do with the mental happenings that usually accompany them, and that pairing is knowable only by independent confirmation of the mental happenings. This is similar to our knowledge, discussed in the previous chapter, of the correlations between brain states and mental states. This knowledge too requires testimony about mental states to make the right pairings. Testimony is also one of the primary ways we know about the natural world. I've not, for example, studied the fossil record for myself. I take it on the expert testimony of paleontologists that there are many subvarieties of ceratopsian. I know about the weather by the testimony of meteorologists. I know my bank balance by the testimony of the bank. I know what happened in history by the testimony of eyewitnesses. And on and on.

So. Much. Testimony.

Notice, by the way, that believing on the basis of testimony involves a kind of faith in the testifier.

The importance of testimony is why we worry so much about maintaining a free, independent press. It is vital that journalists are not employed or influenced by a particular political party or by some corporation about which they are reporting. Without independence and freedom, we would be unwise to trust that journalists are telling the truth about what's going on in politics or with that corporation. When the press becomes the propaganda wing of some other entity, the evidential value of the press's testimony is dramatically decreased. The point is that we see the vital role that testimony plays in our lives when we consider this point about a free press. No wonder that decreasing confidence in the independence of the media has coincided with, for example, an increase in political cynicism and partisanship.

Testimony is a vital source of evidence and, therefore, knowledge. And if we can know things on the basis of the fallible testimony of finite, fallen human beings, we can most certainly know things on the basis of the testimony of an infinite, perfect God. The Scriptures, as God's written Word to us, are a path to knowledge, no less than the testimony of our parents or of the press. We can know that something is true just by reading it in the Bible.

~◦~

You might be wondering, "Doesn't that just push the question back to whether the Bible really is God's Word?" Great question! The answer is simple: Yes, yes it does! Here's the thing, though. I don't intend to defend the claim that the Bible is God's Word. As I've already said, I'm just taking that for granted. It's the view of the Christian, and I'm concerned with what the person who is already devoted to Jesus ought to think about whether you can know just because the Bible says so. If you want a defense of the truth of Christianity, and of the claim that the Bible is divine testimony, you'll search this book in vain. I'm here to show what you should think supposing you're already devoted to Christ and to show you where the culture is going wrong.[7] Let's just move right along then.

~❦~

Beyond our tendency toward scientism, there is another reason we find it difficult to trust God's testimony in the Bible. The evidence of our eyes and ears, and the evidence of our fallen minds, is prone to lie to us about who God is and what he is doing in the world. We need the Scriptures to open our eyes and ears and minds to the truth. This is a consistent witness of heroes of the Christian faith.

Take Corrie ten Boom. I recommend everyone read her fantastic little autobiography *The Hiding Place*, or her letters from prison.[8] Better, read both. For a quick overview, you can have a look at the chapter on Corrie and the rest of the ten Boom family in Jim Belcher's *In Search of Deep Faith* or in Eric Metaxas's *Seven Women*.[9] Corrie's family worked tirelessly to protect Jews from the Nazis during World War II. They were eventually found out, and Corrie and her sister Betsie wound up in Nazi concentration camps.

But even Corrie struggled to see the world as it is. In fact, there are a number of remarkable occasions on which Corrie's sister Betsie corrects her vision. Here's one. Corrie and Betsie discovered during their imprisonment at Vught that a man named Jan Vogel had betrayed the ten Boom family to the Gestapo. Corrie was enraged. "Flames of fire," she wrote, "seemed to lead around that name in my heart. . . . I knew that if Jan Vogel stood in front of me now, I could kill him."[10] Corrie felt, as I do at far less egregious wrongs, that the man who destroyed her family and its work was deserving of vengeance, not mercy. Betsie, however, "seemed to carry no burden of rage," a fact that struck Corrie.[11] Corrie reports interrogating Betsie: "Betsie, don't you feel anything about Jan Vogel? Doesn't it bother you?" Betsie's reply is jarring. "Oh yes,

Corrie! Terribly! I've felt for him ever since I knew—and pray for him whenever his name comes into my mind. How dreadfully he must be suffering!" Corrie was shaken. She couldn't sleep. "Once again," she writes, "I had the feeling that this sister with whom I had spent all my life belonged somehow to another order of beings. Wasn't she telling me in her gentle way that I was as guilty as Jan Vogel? Didn't he and I stand together before an all-seeing God convicted of the same sin of murder? For I had murdered him with my heart and with my tongue." Betsie was teaching Corrie to see the world as Jesus would have us see it, as a place where those of us who harbor contempt or hatred for our fellow image bearers are guilty of murder. Betsie could see this truth; and she helped Corrie to see it, too.

Corrie and Betsie eventually wound up at Ravensbruck. Their barracks, Barracks 28, was overcrowded, squalid, disgusting. Their straw bunks were infested with fleas. Betsie, somehow, insisted that she and Corrie thank God for their new situation. Betsie wanted to be faithful to Paul's command to the Thessalonians to give thanks in all circumstances. I have to imagine she was also thinking about Paul's insistence that "we know that in all things God works for the good of those who love him" (Rom. 8:28), a claim that, as I mentioned earlier, often strikes me as incredible bordering on ridiculous. Not Betsie. Corrie recounts Betsie's prayer:

> "Thank you," Betsie went on serenely, "for the fleas and for—"
> The fleas! This was too much. "Betsie, there's no way even God can make me grateful for a flea." "Give thanks in *all* circumstances," she quoted. "It doesn't say, 'in pleasant circumstances.' Fleas are part of this place where God has put us."[12]

Corrie and Betsie went on to do amazing things in those barracks.

Side by side, in the sanctuary of God's fleas, Betsie and I minis-
tered the Word of God to all in the room. We sat by deathbeds that
became doorways of heaven. We watched women who had lost
everything grow rich in hope. The knitters of Barracks 28 became
the praying heart of the vast diseased body that was Ravensbruck,
interceding for all in the camp—guards, under Betsie's prodding,
as well as prisoners. We prayed beyond the concrete walls for the
healing of Germany, of Europe, of the world.[13]

This ministry took place under the noses of the Nazis, and without
any interference whatever. Later in Betsie's and Corrie's time there,
Betsie discovered why they were allowed to continue unhindered:
it was the fleas. The guards wouldn't enter Barracks 28 because of
the fleas. Here's how Corrie describes her reaction to this news:
"I remembered Betsie's bowed head, remembered her thanks to
God for creatures I could see no use for."[14] Betsie could see what
Corrie couldn't. Betsie saw with the eyes of the kingdom. And she
was able to do this because she trusted the Scriptures and gave herself to what God reveals in them.

I'm making a simple point: the Bible says things that strike us
as ridiculous, but we have a God who is in the business of making
the ridiculous into reality. Especially when we are confronted with
great suffering and sorrow, it is imperative that we bathe our hearts
in stories of God's redemptive habits. Ours is a God who used the
cruelty of Joseph's brothers, and I suppose the arrogance of Joseph
himself, to save his people from famine. He is a God who chose
Moses, an inarticulate murderer, to represent him before the most
powerful king of the ancient world. He is a God who redeems the
world through crucifixion, perhaps the most heinous torture imple-
ment ever devised by fallen humanity. God is a God of surprise.

I think this is no small part of why God has given us the Scriptures. Our eyes deceive us, in part because they are fallen, but no

less because we are finite and can therefore only see small glimpses of the whole fabric of reality. It reminds me of a type of image, "photographic mosaics" they're sometimes called, constructed out of much smaller images that serve as pixels, of a sort, for the composite whole. I saw one once, a portrait of Barack Obama. The majority of Obama's face was composed of emoji. Say what you want about Obama, at least he's a serious human being, a man to be reckoned with. But imagine all you could see was one of the mosaic's pixels, one little fist-bump emoji, say. It'd be tough to take that seriously. Fist-bump emojis have far less gravitas, far less dignity, than Barack Obama. Our lives, as important as they are, are sort of like that fist-bump emoji, woven together with other ridiculous pieces to construct a far more serious and beautiful and complicated whole. But we finite humans, little fist-bump emojis that we are, can't see the whole without help. The Scriptures give us that bigger picture.

One regret I have looking back on 2006, and this is why I'm talking about all this here, is that I didn't immerse myself in stories of Christian heroes. I think that would have helped me see my way through to the end of the tunnel, as they say. Why didn't I do that? I don't know. Probably for lots of reasons. But partly it was because I didn't know I should. I didn't know that immersion in those stories could help me see the face of God emerge from my little fist-bump-emoji life.

It's fair to say of me, back then, that I persisted in two interrelated mistakes. First, I thought that the aim of the Scriptures was simply to communicate truths, and second, I believed that these truths were "private" in the sense discussed above. It's also fair to say that these mistakes were likely born from an embrace of the heart-mind dichotomy I discussed back in chapter 2. But the dichotomy had a twist, in my case: unlike *The Bachelorette*, I preferred the mind

to the heart. And this allowed my emotions and longings to discon-
nect from my knowledge of the great truths of the gospel.

What I needed was more, not less. Of course I needed those
great truths of the gospel. Without them, I would be unable to approach the throne of God. And of course the Scriptures communicate truths. Deep, important, abiding truths that ought to function
as the foundation of my life and yours. This is an absolutely vital
role that the Scriptures play for us. The Scriptures are the primary
way we can know about who God is and what he has done, is doing,
and will do with his creation. This is something we simply cannot
forget. When God testifies to the truth, we must listen, and we must
assimilate that truth into our minds.

But the Scriptures do far, far more than communicate truths.
They are not simply a fancy super-science textbook, designed to tell
us how to make predictions about the future or to understand how
the world works. They don't do less, they do more. The Scriptures
paint a picture of God and his world, they embed the great truths of
God, of humanity, and of human history in a story that reaches *all*
of our hearts, not just our minds. They show us the paths we must
walk, through both heroes and villains. They place us within the
grand story of God's creation, give us a history and a family. They
tell a story and show us how that story is *ours*.

This was a crucial insight for me, and so it's one I want to emphasize. My warped desire that the truths of Christianity "work"
in a certain way, where what that means is that it will help me get
what I want, dovetails with the idea that science is the only path to
knowledge. The idea that the truth must be useful is already pointing toward scientism, and the idea that religious truth must work is
part of the sense in which it is private. To elevate modern science
above other forms of knowing is to elevate truths that help us master
and possess nature. We then begin to think of religious truth along
those same lines, and so religious truths begin to be measured by

how well they help me become who I want to be. Whether religious claims are actually *true* needn't arise; the point of religion has become private to me, subject to my own goals and aspirations.[15]

In many ways, the antidote to this tangle is storytelling. Good stories make asking questions about usefulness seem somehow unimportant. Let me try to explain what I mean.

A few months ago, my mom came to visit with her mom, my grandma, my children's great-grandma, Grandma Dorothy. As I'm writing this, Grandma Dorothy is descending deeper into the chaos of dementia. This trip from San Antonio to Los Angeles was a kind of farewell not just for us and Grandma Dorothy, but for her and her brother. The siblings hadn't seen each other in years, and Grandma Dorothy wanted one last time to be with him. We didn't know at the time, but he was dying during their visit. Stage 4 cancer. Anyway, my mom brought letters with her on that trip, letters she and her grandpa—Grandma Dorothy's dad, my children's great-great grandfather—had written to one another many years ago. These letters are precious to my mother. She had rediscovered them during a recent move, and she was treasuring again the memories of their tender relationship. I know what this is like, though maybe in a more muted way. I have this box where I keep all the notes Jamie has written to me over the years, and these days it's beginning to fill up with cards and notes from Lyle and Gretchen too. Seeing my mom reading these letters made me revisit that box not long ago. I think if our house were burning to the ground, the thing I'd try hardest to save—after I knew my children, my wife, and my dog were safe—would be that box. Its value is immeasurable. It contains the physical manifestation of our relationships. Stories. Reminders of love and affection. Encouragement. Simple notes that say little more than hello. My guess is my mom feels similarly about those letters from her grandfather. They remind her of truths long forgotten, but they do far more than that too. More, not less.

This is what the Scriptures are, in a way. Letters from our Father in heaven, given to us with love, for both our instruction in the truth and our shaping into members of his family. There is truth there, no doubt. But more than that, too. The Scriptures are an instrument of change for our whole hearts, including our intellect. More than truth, not less, most often embedded in stories about God and his people.

It shouldn't surprise us that God's decision to use these methods of communication was quite the stroke of genius. Stories shape us. It's difficult to incorporate any truth into the depths of our hearts, much less the hard truths of the wisdom of God, truths that inevitably seem like folly to our fallen minds, when those truths are disconnected from compelling stories. Bare statements of these truths—that God's power is perfected in our weakness, that death is the beginning of life, that true love is revealed in sacrifice—strike us, quite frankly, as ridiculous. But when we see them expressed in beautiful ways in the life of great heroes, or when we see the destruction that comes from rejecting those truths, they somehow seep into our hearts (and so into our minds). I suspect they do so because stories couple mind and emotion, and that leads us to desire. As C. S. Lewis once put, stories have the power to "steal past those watchful dragons" stationed in our hearts.[16]

During my doctoral program, and especially so in 2006, I did not take this seriously. Well, maybe that's a bit harsh on my younger self. This at least was true: I didn't read the Bible to have my whole heart shaped. I looked to the Scriptures only for truth. I had a truncated understanding of the Bible, and so a truncated understanding of what it meant to read the Bible well. I needed to give myself not only to the study of the truths of Scripture, but to the *story itself*. The story includes the truths, of course. More, not less. No surprise that my growth into Christlikeness and my trust in Jesus for what I truly needed were truncated as well. In other words, part of my problem was a limited imagination, specifically with respect to what God might be doing in the Scriptures.

To read the Scriptures well is to read them in light of the fullness of what they do to us. They communicate truth, to be sure, but they also communicate God's love more fully, in the way that I try to communicate my love for my children not just with my words but also through my embrace. More, not less. Giving yourself in this way places questions of usefulness in their proper location. It may be that my embrace of Lyle serves some utilitarian function. But that's not really the point. The point is just the embrace itself. The connection it embodies. Our goal is to abide with God, not use him as a tool like a scientist in her lab.

So we must immerse our hearts in the stories of Scripture, starting of course with the story of Jesus. But we must embrace the other stories as well, of the Garden, of Abraham, of the Exodus, of David and Solomon, of Isaiah and Jeremiah and Jonah and Hosea, of Peter and Paul and John, and of all the great heroes of God since. We must drink them in, so that we might know with our whole hearts the love of God in Christ Jesus our Lord, and so that we might sharpen our vision as we hunt for God. More. Not less.

⁓❧

One brief afterthought, an application of the earlier points about suffering. Reckoning with sin, both confessing it to others and battling it until it dies, is psychologically unpleasant, to say the least. It feels a lot like, and sometimes maybe just is, a form of suffering. To not sin when one wants to sin is to not get what one desires, and unfulfilled desire is a form of suffering. In other words, becoming like Jesus involves suffering. But it's productive suffering. There's this old movie called *The Shawshank Redemption*. It's primarily about Andy Dufrense, a prisoner at Shawshank State Penitentiary, wrongly convicted for murdering his wife and her lover.

Toward the end of the film, Dufrense escapes to freedom through the sewer of the prison. Battling sin feels a lot like what Dufrense must have felt as he stepped out of his clean, well-kept, tidy cell and into that pipe of human excrement. It's often through the muck that we find freedom.

Chapter 8 Discussion Questions

- Can you think of anything that, to your surprise, you know only because of testimony?
- Are there any biblical teachings that you struggle to believe are actually true?
- When was the last time reading the Bible caused you to change your mind about something?
- Can we know things that we've only read in the Bible?

CHAPTER 9

Can We Maintain Christian Belief in a Pluralistic World?

In the last chapter, I mentioned two reasons why faithfulness is so hard. I hope I didn't give the impression that these were the only two reasons. There are lots of reasons why faithfulness is so hard these days (and any days, really). I was only dealing with two currently prominent ones. Here's some evidence that the list of two wasn't meant to be exhaustive: this chapter is about a third reason!

One of the disorienting things about studying philosophy is that no one agrees about anything. In fact, there really aren't any significant claims or principles about which philosophers agree. Even basic principles of logic are disputed. Take, for example, the "law of noncontradiction," which says that no claim can be both true and false (at the same time and in the same sense). You might think that's undeniable. I mean, if it's raining outside, it can't also be *not* raining! But there's a whole branch of logic devoted to so-called "paraconsistent" systems, logics that deny the law of noncontradiction. I really mean it: in philosophy, anything goes! In light of this, one of my professors said once that in philosophy all you can really hope to establish are conditionals. By that he meant that all you could hope to show is that *if* one thing is true, *then* something else is too. And you can do that without having a view about the one thing, or even if you think that one thing is false. Unlike chess, where you must start with your pieces positioned in a certain way, in philosophy you can put your pieces anywhere you like to begin the game, and you only need to worry about what moves you can make given where they started. Philosophy is therefore happily pluralistic: different philosophers believe incompatible things, and we've learned to get along despite those differences.

This reminds me of a moment during my dissertation defense. My committee and I were sitting around the conference table in Waggener Hall room 316. They were, as they were meant to be, peppering me with pointed questions about my project. Josh Dever took his turn. He said something like this: "I'd like to talk about footnote 46 on page 98." This was trouble. I had buried a rather crucial move, one that I didn't quite know how to defend, in that footnote. And I was hoping no one would read the notes. I should've known. Josh and I went back and forth a bit, and I owned up to the fact that I didn't have an *argument* for the premise that I needed to make the argument of that footnote work. Josh was reassuring: eventually philosophy hits bedrock, moments where the arguments give out, and this felt enough like bedrock for him to excuse me from the need for arguments. It would be an understatement to say that I was relieved. Josh couldn't care less whether what I was saying was actually *true*. He only cared that I'd gotten deep enough down to appropriately ground my movements from one place to another. Josh's is a generous sort of pluralism, and my experience was of that generous pluralism in action.

Philosophical pluralism raises a profound and difficult question: Is there any hope for philosophical *knowledge*? If anything goes, how could we possibly know that some particular philosophical claim is *true*?

It's a short step to an even deeper, more existentially troubling question. Given that philosophy can't really be quarantined from ethics, and ethics can't be quarantined from religion, this question about philosophy becomes a question about ethics and about religion: Is ethical and religious knowledge really possible? This is a question not just for philosophers. It's a question for Christians. All Christians. Especially Christians who have friends—smart, well-intentioned, honest friends—who aren't Christians. So it is a question for my children no less than my students, all of whom have non-Christian friends. I suspect this is true for almost every Christian. If it's not, it at least ought to be, since we are called as a church to take the gospel of Jesus to everyone everywhere.

⁓✲

This question about whether ethical and religious knowledge is possible plagued me during 2006 in a way that I didn't realize until later. It was a question that I rarely considered consciously. When it did come explicitly to mind, I was rather dismissive of it. I would think, What difference does it make that people disagree with me? I'm doing my best to follow the evidence! But I did feel, existentially, worries about whether I was rational to keep going to church, to keep going to Bible studies, to keep praying, to keep endeavoring to orient my relationships around Jesus. A part of the challenge, I now think, had to do with the fact that I was spending significant amounts of time with the smartest people I'd ever known, and they had wildly divergent views about the basic contours of reality. Some were committed Christians, some were vaguely theistic with no real religious commitment, some were agnostic, and some were rabidly atheistic. Deep down, this pluralistic environment troubled me. It made me worry that none of us were rational to keep on believing as we did, since so many smart, capable, learned people disagreed with us.

Now, I don't mean to give away the punchline, but I don't think philosophical, ethical, and religious skepticism are warranted just by the facts of pluralism.

I do, though, want to emphasize how serious a problem this is. First, there's the distinctly intellectual concern. My dismissive attitude—I'm following the evidence!—was unwarranted for precisely the reason that I used to defend the claim that you can know stuff just by reading the Bible: testimony is a source of evidence, even knowledge. Pluralism is implictly testimonial. I mean that in a pluralistic environment, if you're aware of the pluralism then you're aware that smart, well-meaning people disagree with you. That knowledge functions as a sort of testimony to the credibility of views opposed to Christianity. The fact, if it is one, that none of them have ever uttered their disagreement to you doesn't really matter. Anyway, I was in a position where I had, in conversation, explicitly disagreed with my professors on religious issues. I had, on many occasions, had polite but frank conversations with them about my views and theirs. They had given me testimony that I was wrong. If that testimony is what I said it was in the previous chapter, there's real trouble lurking here.

Okay, so that's a first pass at the problem: pluralism is testimony that Christianity is false, and testimony is good evidence. As I've already mentioned, it's a problem that I confronted more or less every day during my time in my PhD program. And it took a toll, I think. That's not a bad thing! I'm grateful now that my experience at UT forced me to confront this issue head on. No doubt some of the challenge was not particularly intellectual. It's difficult to reckon with the fact that some of your closest friends are simply wrong regarding the deepest and most important facts about reality. I would have preferred to give myself to the idea that Christianity was really a private matter, and in that way avoid the need to have real disagreements with my friends. I knew better, though; I knew that view just wasn't sustainable, despite its existential allure.

There are serious intellectual concerns here as well. In many cases, when we're confronted with smart people who disagree with us about a question, and who we think have all the evidence that we do, it seems like we ought to withhold judgment on the question until we've had a chance to reflect more carefully on the matter. Here's a simple case, one that's used a lot in the academic conversation about this issue. Imagine you're at dinner with two of your closest friends. You've been going out with these two friends every week for years, and you always just split the check three ways; you figure over time all the meal-to-meal imbalances in cost will even out, and it's easier to just split it anyway. One thing you've learned over all these meals is that your friends are just as good at math as you are, and all three of you are pretty good at math. Usually, you just do it in your respective heads. Maybe twice a year, you get it wrong. Same for them. And there's really no pattern. Sometimes you get it wrong and they don't, sometimes one of them gets it wrong and you don't, sometimes (though more rarely) two of you get it wrong but the third doesn't, etcetera. Now imagine you're at dinner one week, and you do the math in your head. Adding a 20 percent tip, you figure each of the three shares is $17.50. You believe, on the basis of the high-quality evidence your mental calculations constitute, that each share is $17.50. But after you've announced your conclusion, both of your friends, having done the math in their heads, claim that each share is $16.50.

What's the rational response here? What I mean is, how should you revise your beliefs in light of the fact that your friends disagree with you while agreeing with one another? Should you persist in your view that each share is $17.50? Probably not. You know your friends are just as good at calculating as you are, and it's pretty unlikely that they'd get the same conclusion unless they were right. That you disagree with the pair of them who got the same answer looks like pretty good evidence that you made a calculation error. No doubt you would break out your phone's calculators to settle the matter conslusively, but in the meantime, it seems irrational for you to go on believing each share is $17.50. You should at best be agnostic between the two candidate answers, and you should maybe even weakly believe that each share is $16.50. So this is a case in which it looks like disagreeing with an intellectual equal who has roughly the same evidence as you makes persisting in your belief irrational.

The problem we must confront is that religious pluralism similarly seems to render religious belief irrational. Smart, well-meaning, intellectually honest people who have gathered lots of evidence on religious matters, evidence that seems just as good as yours and mine, disagree with us on whether Christianity is true. Doesn't that mean, like in the case of the restaurant check, that we should suspend our belief in Christianity until we can manage to find some "religion calculator" to check our work? And given that we don't have one of those, and that one doesn't seem to be forthcoming, doesn't that mean that we aren't rational to keep on believing that Christianity is true?

I won't pretend that I'm going to solve this whole problem in one chapter. But I want to at least point toward a path that I think leads to a solution. Bear with me for a bit . . .

~❦~

Solomon's opening gambit in the book of Proverbs contains a rather surprising claim: "The fear of the LORD is the beginning of knowledge" (1:7). I say this is surprising because we tend not to think of fear as relevant to the sort of wisdom-grounding knowledge Solomon is picturing in his proverbs. What has fear to do with, to pick a random example, Proverbs 10:17, "Whoever heeds discipline shows the way to life, but whoever ignores correction leads others astray"? Solomon seems to be suggesting that you can't *really* arrive at a full understanding of that seemingly simple teaching without first fearing the Lord. I would encourage you to reflect on this, on Solomon's claim that fear of God is the first stop along the path to knowledge. I bring it up to make just one observation: there is some sort of connection between our emotions and our intellect. If our emotions are disordered, so will be our minds.

This insight has been picked up over the centuries. Plato believed that a person can't know what she doesn't love. Jonathan Edwards contended that "true benevolence," a sort of enlightening of the whole heart, including our desires and emotions, was essential to communion with God. This idea has fallen out of favor in many circles, replaced with a detached ideal of pure mathematical rationality, one that is almost robotic in its proper application. But the older view is resilient, and is I think making a comeback. Take Kelly Kapic, one of my favorite contemporary theologians. Reflecting on his own encounters with the tension between his Christian faith and his experiences of pain and suffering, he asserts that "benevolence and truth are meant to nourish one another."[1]

Solomon doesn't elaborate on the idea that the fear of God is the beginning of knowledge. Here's one thought about why the connection might make sense. Fear primes us to notice certain aspects of our surroundings and to ignore others. As my family knows, I have a terrible fear of falling, and an even greater fear of one of my children falling! I remember a number of times standing near the edge of the grassy bluff outside Fort Ebey on Whidbey Island, watching Lyle and Gretchen enjoy the summer sun setting in red and gold between the Olympic Peninsula and Vancouver Island. Usually the fear of one of them—especially Gretchen, since Lyle has always been a bit more stable on his feet—tumbling over the edge toward the rocky beach below distracted me from the beauty of the sunset. Unlike my obliviousness to the sunset, I was keenly aware of the spots where long grass might be hiding the edge of the bluff. My fear kept me focused on that aspect of the environment. Whether this fear was (is?!) rational or not, the point is just that my experience of fear shaped my attention.

Psychologist Barbara Frederickson has done fascinating work on emotions, especially positive emotions. Her theory has come to be called the "broaden and build" theory.[2] The basic idea is that positive emotions, emotions like happiness and enjoyment, tend to broaden one's awareness of one's surroundings. As a result, Frederickson has shown, people who experience more positive emotions tend to be more creative, more resilient, more able to grasp the "big picture." It's easy to see how this might work when you contrast it with negative emotions like fear. Negative emotions tend to narrow your awareness, just like my awareness gets hyper-focused on that Whidbey cliff when I fear that Gretchen will fall. Frederickson, in other words, has shown how emotions shape what we notice in our experience and in the world. And what we notice becomes evidence that we use to discern the truth. Emotions, at the very least, impact our beliefs in this way: emotions shape our evidence.[3]

Back to Solomon. What might we expect from someone who fears God? What sorts of things might such a person notice about herself, other people, her environment, the wider world, the universe as a whole? The first thing to expect is that, like the person who fears falling, her attention will be drawn to different aspects of reality than the person who doesn't fear God. She might notice, for example, her own frailty, her own finitude, her own brokenness. Why? Because when we are confronted with fear, the object of our fear tends to loom large in our minds. So the one who fears God might, for example, compare herself first to God rather than to other creatures. And in that comparison, we are frail, small, and broken.[4]

But the person who fears God might also be more likely to discern God's activity in the world. She might notice God's care for her in times of trouble or despair, and she might sense God's grace toward her own brokenness and sin. These might couple fear of God to joy. And that joy, which involves (but is not exhausted by) positive emotions, will alert her to the bigger picture of things, to what God is doing and what role even present suffering and difficulty might play in God's plans. The positive emotions that couple with an embrace of God, in other words, might help a person embrace her challenges and struggles as "light and momentary troubles," as Paul put it (2 Cor. 4:17).

There is, no doubt, far more to say about the psychology of all this, about the ways that an embrace of the gospel and of God affect our emotions and in turn our evidence. But I hope the point is clear: emotions, at the very least, position us to encounter certain evidence. Since what is reasonable to believe will depend on what evidence we have, what it is reasonable to believe will depend in part on the contours of our emotional life. Notice, crucially and more specifically, that fear of God is likely to impact an individual's sensitivity to God's presence. That's crucial. I beg you to keep it in mind for a moment.

~~&

How is all this relevant to the problem of pluralism? It's fairly simple really. For pluralism to create a real problem for the rationality of our Christian belief, we must think that the pluralism case is sufficiently like the restaurant check case. That requires thinking that Christians and non-Christians will have comparable, equally good evidence about whether Christianity is true. But the thing is, our religious commitments shape our emotions. And our emotions in turn shape our evidence. And so it's not at all obvious that Christians and non-Christians are sufficiently like the friends in the restaurant check case. Maybe, in other words, Christians and non-Christians are not after all equally well-positioned to evaluate the truth of Christianity. Not because non-Christians are irrational or something, much less because *Christians* are irrational, but just because Christians have access to evidence that their non-Christian friends don't, evidence only available to those with a certain sort of emotional life.

Now, I want to be clear: I don't take what I've just said to supply a full-blown solution to the problem posed by religious pluralism, by disagreement about religious claims. It's really just the first step. What I really wanted to do is point out that it's not at all obvious—in fact, there are reasons to doubt—that Christians and non-Christians are equally well-positioned to evaluate the truth of Christianity. So far, those reasons come just from reflecting on the way emotions might shape our attention. That's something that you don't have to be a Christian to embrace.

⁓

There are also distinctively Christian reasons to think the playing field is uneven as well, reasons that aren't all too distinct from my gambit about emotions.

If Christianity is true, the story of the world is really quite simple. Theologians tend to summarize it in four words, four vital moments in the unfolding of the story of the world: *creation, Fall, redemption, consummation*. The story begins "In the beginning" (Gen. 1). God is there, and he creates all that exists apart from himself. Light and darkness, heavens and earth, land and sea. All of it is created good by this good God. And the final act of creation is the creation of humanity, Adam and Eve, to tend and care for God's good world, the world God loves. Creation. The next part of the story, the Fall, is the tragic bit. Adam and Eve rebel against God, rejecting his authority and his rule, setting themselves up in his place. God curses both them and the creation. Fall. But God doesn't stop loving creation and especially can't stop loving humanity. Despite the continual rebellion of men and women the world over, God works to restore them to relationship. First, God chooses Abraham to make a family that will bless and ultimately redeem all humanity.

Then, into Abraham's line God sends Jesus, the incarnation of his Son, to complete that redemption. Through his life, death, resurrection, and ascension, Jesus makes a way for us to be admitted into the very presence of God. Redemption. And yet there is work left to do. God's work is not fully manifest. It has not been consummated. This is what we still await, the final return of heaven to earth and the making new of all things. This is our hope: the final victory of Jesus over sin and death, and life with him forever in the heavenly city on the new earth. Consummation.

That's the story of this world. I like to think this story can be understood fundamentally in terms of the way God's love unfolds in history. So the Creation-Fall-Redemption-Consummation story is really a story about divine love. What I mean is that each of those four moments in the story of the world ought to be understood through the love of God. Take creation. Creation is a story of God's love. The God of Christianity is not needy. He did not create the world, nor humanity in it, to give him something that he didn't have but needed. God's life in himself is one of perfect Trinitarian love. There is no lack. God creates in order to share this love, to bless. In creating, God can give himself away. Creation is for love. I won't talk here about how the other parts of the story, even perhaps surprisingly the story of the Fall, are likewise ordered by love. That's for another book.

I do, though, want to say something about how this story, specifically the story of the Fall, relates to the challenge of religious pluralism. One of the results of the Fall, maybe one of the most important parts, is the effect it has on our minds. It's not just that we *want* the wrong things, or even that we *will* the wrong things, but that we *believe* the wrong things. Our hearts and minds, as Paul puts it, are "foolish" and "darkened" (Rom. 1:21). We "suppress the truth by [our] wickedness" (Rom. 1:18) and so choose to worship the wrong things, created things rather than our Creator. Truth suppression—which comes along with the Fall—leads to idolatry.

Of course, when the Scriptures were being penned, the primary form of idolatry was *literal*. People made statues and worshipped fake gods they took those statues to represent. They made up beings and made them more important than God. Our idols aren't so obvious, or anyway they aren't so literal. We worship money, physical health and beauty, economic success and the stuff we can buy with it, leisure, sports teams, and sex. That's not an exhaustive list, of course. The nonobviousness of our idols doesn't render them less pernicious or destructive. Maybe they're even worse: because they aren't obvious, it's easier to fool ourselves into thinking they aren't really idols.

This aspect of the Fall, the way that suppressing knowledge leads to idolatry, is the flip side of the way that knowledge transforms us and leads us to worship, of the idea that we must add knowledge to our faith, of all the good things that knowledge does for us as Christians. The Fall, it turns out, warps our minds as well.

In fact, the Fall of humanity was rooted in an act of demonic deception. It was a lie that led our first ancestors astray. God had told Adam and Eve to avoid eating the fruit of a particular tree. If you "eat from it," he said, "you will certainly die" (Gen. 2:17). The serpent demurred. He made Eve wonder whether God was right. He told her, "You will not certainly die" (Gen. 3:4). This subtle deception made Eve question God's judgment about the tree and led her to act in direct opposition to God. She ate the fruit and gave it to Adam to eat as well. Adam ate alongside Eve. The serpent's lie created the space for Adam and Eve to set themselves up as masters of good and evil. They elevated themselves to a place where only God belongs. The first idolatrous act any humans ever committed. Because the Fall is rooted in deception, it's no surprise that the Fall brings with it intellectual consequences.

Back to religious pluralism. The challenge is to explain how smart, seemingly well-meaning and intellectually honest people could consider the evidence for Christianity and reject it. What we've just seen, though, is that the Christian story *predicts* this fact. It says, in effect, that fallen humans will suppress their knowledge of God and replace him with idols of their own making. This is just what fallen humanity does. The process is not always concious or deliberate, any more than Adam and Eve could be said to consciously and deliberately construct an idol. This sort of suppression and idolatry can also be communal, passed down from generation to generation. So it needn't be something that each individual generated wholly on his or her own. It might be passed on from parents to children, for example; I suspect this is very often the case. It is suppression and idolatry nonetheless.

Importantly, the Fall is part of the core logic of the Christian story. It's not just an add-on to explain religious pluralism. It's not really there to explain religious pluralism *at all*. It's there to explain what's wrong with the world and why God has to do so much to fix things. That the Fall winds up predicting religious pluralism is striking, though, since it shows that Christianity is not really at odds with the facts of religious pluralism. That smart, seemingly well-meaning and intellectually honest people reject Christianity is what you would expect to find *if Christianity is in fact true*. What would conflict with Christianity is a world full of nothing but Christians!

~*

I really do believe all of that. But, to be honest, I find it a bit incredible. I find it odd that Christianity predicts a world full of smart, well-meaning non-Christians. I find it odd that Christianity forces me to say that seemingly well-meaning and intellectually honest people are suppressing the truth. Strangely, though, I don't find it odd at all to suggest that every human being whatsoever is a broken mess, and that this brokenness no doubt has an intellectual component. Which is to say, my feelings on this issue are a bit of a mess themselves. I suspect many people, including many Christians, feel similarly. Pulled in two directions at once.

So I suppose we're confronted with a choice. Do we trust that the Scriptures are right about all this, that we all tend to suppress the truth and to worship created things? This suppression means that despite what we might think even of ourselves, we're each prone—like Adam and Eve were in the beginning—to elevating ourselves above God and to resisting what we would otherwise know: that God exists and has shown himself to us in the person of Jesus. This is existentially challenging, even if it's intellectually sufficient. I'm not sure that I'll ever really find it easy to suggest that my friends and neighbors who don't love Jesus are suppressing the truth. I've found it difficult since at least 2006, and I don't see any reason to think the difficulty will wane. It certainly hasn't yet.

However, it is a comfort to know that we can accept this explanation of religious pluralism without pride or arrogance, since we Christians are no less guilty of truth suppression than anyone else. Even those of us who trust in Jesus resist God and his truth in ways similar to non-Christians. But for the grace of God, we would be similarly in the dark. So it is no credit to me that I believe in Jesus. The same for all of us. Credit goes to God alone, who must continually give us grace to believe.

Chapter 9 Discussion Questions

- Do you have many non-Christian friends? How important to you is it that they begin following Jesus?
- What are different reasons why non-Christians prompt you or people you know to question the truth of Christianity?
- How have you experienced the Fall's effects on your intellect? Can you think of a silly or comical example? A serious or important example?
- Is it rational to be a Christian in a pluralistic world?

Epilogue

CHAPTER 10

The Way Forward

A funny thing has happened as I've written this book. I started writing because I thought I had an answer to a question, a question I needed to answer to move through those struggles that came to a head in spring 2006, a question that I believe other Christians need to answer as well. The question is about why knowledge matters to those who are already devoted to Jesus. Why should we keep endeavoring to know more and more about God and his creation? The answer is simple, and obvious once you notice it: we need knowledge in order to move ever deeper into the life of God, since knowledge about God facilitates and supports knowledge of God. That still seems right to me.

As I've written, however, I've come to a different realization. I hinted at this back in chapter 6, where I first described the connection between knowledge about God and knowledge of him. Here is the realization stated baldly: there's a sense in which all Christians, young and old, already have all the knowledge anyone ever needs. It's knowledge that any child can have, and indeed it's knowledge enshrined in a classic Sunday school song: "Jesus loves me, this I know, for the Bible tells me so." That's really all you need. The same thing is true of our knowledge of the Creation-Fall-Redemption-

Consummation narrative. That's a simple story, again one that even children can comprehend. What I mean is that the main contours of the story of the world are straightforward, easy to understand, and the gospel of Jesus is equally easy to understand. I know the story. And so do my children and my students. So do you. And knowing the story, which is really just another way of telling the gospel, and entrusting yourself to the Author of that story is all we must do. And yet . . .

~&

And yet there's so much more to learn and discover and understand.

What has struck me about this realization is that, in a certain sense, it requires a fundamental altering of my perspective on the importance of knowledge and how I should order my intellectual life. In a way, in 2006, and really up until recently, I believed that Jesus had yet to give me enough. There was something else I *needed*. And what I needed was at least in part more knowledge. But that, when put so plainly, is just ridiculous. Jesus had already given me *himself*, and along with himself he had given me access to the Father and had sent his Spirit to dwell within me. I already knew that gift, that person. What more could I possibly need?

A radical reorientation is in order. I know the story and that's all I really need. But all the while everything I've written must stay in place. I realize that sounds rather strange. Knowledge does lead to worship and formation, and ultimately to God's presence. So we must pursue knowledge. Put another way: somehow there's a sense in which I'm still learning it and still need to learn it, despite already knowing it. That's funny. And I want to explore how we might make sense of this tension and what it means for us as Jesus followers.

There's a story I heard once about Karl Barth. Barth was arguably the most important Christian theologian of the twentieth century. His magnum opus is the *Church Dogmatics*, a systematic theology in four volumes, written over thirty-five years. It's massive, somewhere in the neighborhood of 6,000,000 words. Six. *Million*. Words. Just to compare, this book totals just north of 46,000 words. The four volumes of Barth's *Dogmatics* are so long that it's often published in twelve volumes. (Ted Lasso once asked of Great Britain, How many countries are in this country? With the *Church Dogmatics* the question is, How many books are in this book?) Many theologians place Barth in the pantheon of the most important theologians in Christian history, alongside Augustine, Aquinas, Calvin, and maybe a couple of others. I confess I don't share this level of enthusiasm for Barth, but there can be no doubt that Barth's theological work is in many respects masterful and in every respect formidable. No matter your view, theology as it is practiced today is theology practiced in Barth's shadow. Barth, like him or not, is a force.

Back to the story. Barth went on a speaking tour in the United States in 1962. He was Swiss, and international travel, especially intercontinental travel, was rare at that time. As you might expect, this was a rather big deal. People came out in droves to hear him. At each venue, he would give his presentation, and afterward he would take questions. During one Q&A session, a seminary student asked Barth if he could summarize his entire theology in a single sentence. Now, you might expect someone of Barth's stature to bristle at this sort of request, or at least to struggle. I mean, how can you condense 6,000,000 words—some 20,000 pages in a typical contemporary word processor—into a single sentence? Barth was evidently un-intimidated and responded: "Yes: Jesus loves me, this I know, for the Bible tells me so."

One of the most sophisticated and subtle theologians of the last century, maybe even ever, summarized his theology by reciting a Sunday school mantra. Barth believed his theology was, in a deep and important sense, no more sophisticated than the lyrics to a children's song. To understand Barth's view, all you need is the

ability to understand that song. And this is something that more
or less every young child can do. Children can understand Barth.
However, in another equally important sense, children cannot understand Barth. There's a depth and breadth of his thought that is
simply inaccessible to the five-year-old mind. And that is reflected
in Barth's recitation of "Jesus Loves Me." He says those words in a
way that children simply can't. There's a chasm between a spiritually
immature rendition of "Jesus Loves Me" and a spiritually mature
rendition of those same lines. There's a sameness, but it's wrapped
in difference.

~✦

There's an old word that's somewhat out of fashion that I think cap-
tures what I'm trying to get at. The word is *fullness*. What Barth had
but five-year-olds in Sunday school lack is the fullness of the knowledge expressed in "Jesus Loves Me." What we ultimately need—
what *I* need—is fullness, not something new. What we need is to
recognize the fullness of the truth that we are already connected to
God intimately, personally, and without fail. This is not different
from what children know when they sing "Jesus Loves Me." Rather,
it's the deepening and widening of the simple, great truth of the
gospel of Jesus.

I've come to think fullness is what Paul had in mind when he
prayed that the Christians in Ephesus, "being rooted and established in love, may have power . . . to grasp how wide and long
and high and deep is the love of Christ, and to know this love that
suprasses knowledge—that you may be filled to the measure of all
the fullness of God" (Eph. 3:17–19).[1] Paul was praying that those
Ephesian Christians would encounter the fullness of the gospel and
as a result that they would come to be acquainted with the love of
Christ, a love that is both beyond mere propositional knowledge
and better than mere propositional knowledge.

Here's another way to say the same thing. What we need and what I needed all those years ago, and still need today, is not simply more knowledge or different knowledge. What we need is the fullness of what we already know. What I longed for unconsciously in 2006 and consciously today was and is the fullness of the knowledge I already have. That fullness moves us deeper into the Trinitarian life I had already been welcomed into because it shows us the way to encounter the Trinitarian God more fully and deeply, in spirit and in truth.

Fullness is in part a matter of knowledge. It requires individual bits of propositional knowledge. But it requires much more. It requires a certain ordering of our propositional knowledge. We subject our knowledge, and our patterns of investigation, to the gospel of Jesus and the Lordship of Christ. We "take every thought captive" and strive to be "transformed by the renewing of our minds." This is, after all, our "true and proper worship." In this sense, knowledge is not more, or different, or beyond what we already know. It is simply amplification of the great, simple truth of the gospel, of that four-part narrative of the world. So we must strive to relate everything we come to know about God and his world to this gospel and this narrative. As Herman Bavinck once put it, "The mind of the Christian is not satisfied until every form of existence has been referred to the triune God."[2] In this way, we allow our knowledge to connect us to God himself.

So fullness answers the question I longed to answer during my doctoral program. Philosophy matters because it can illuminate the fullness of the gospel, expressed in that four-part narrative. And the fullness of the gospel story also answers all the questions I've been dealing with in these pages. Does Jesus really care about knowledge? Yes: knowledge brings fullness. Is truth objective? Yes: God is Creator, not us. Can our religious beliefs be reasonable? Yes: God is loving, so he instructs rather than manipulates. Is faith compatible with knowledge? Yes: the fullness of faith is born from knowledge (among other things). Can you know anything apart from science? And can you know something just because the Bible says it's so? Yes: God desires our good, and so he speaks in all sorts of ways about himself and his actions. Can you maintain your Christian belief in a pluralistic world? Yes: the gospel predicts that we will suppress the truth in our fallenness, so we should expect a wide number and variety of non-Christians. These answers are all amplifications of the gospel.

More importantly, though, fullness gets the crucial intellectual root of that deeper, existential question about why I found it so difficult to thrive during those years in Texas. The problem is easy to state but tricky to overcome: I hadn't reckoned with the reality that I had everything I needed. The anxiety, the worry, the striving, the perfectionism, the fear of failure. All of that was a denial of the central claim of the gospel: Jesus has given *himself* to me, and Jesus is all I need.

I said earlier that fullness is a matter of knowledge. But it requires more, not less. The more is not merely that ordering of knowledge I already mentioned. Fullness is only achieved through experience. To acquire the fullness of the gospel, we need to experience what we already have. We need to encounter God himself through Jesus Christ, so that we might embrace more deeply and consciously that our lives are "hidden with Christ in God" (Col. 3:3) in our union with our Savior. We need to act out our faith by moving into the holy of holies so that we might experience God in our weakness. Our lives are already hidden with Christ in God. We must embrace that reality experientially. In coming to know God in this way, through the fullness of our knowledge of the gospel, we thereby come to know ourselves. This then allows us to give ourselves away, to become known by others and thereby to give them what they truly need: connection with God.

The Christian's knowledge, what we know, is in an already–not yet state. This is just like our whole lives, and indeed like the whole world. We already have the salvation that we need. And yet we wait to be saved. Jesus has already won the victory over sin and death, and yet we wait for him to establish his reign on earth as it is in heaven. We already have all the knowledge that we need. And yet we need so much more.

⟶⟡

This idea of fullness offers guidance for our intellectual lives. The gospel requires us to subject all things to Christ. As we seek to make sense of politics, or ethics, or education, we look first to the gospel. From there, from the foot of the cross, we inquire. And we always seek, if we are able, to relate what we learn to the basic story of the world. This is deeply freeing. It eliminates the need to strive without destroying the motive to explore.

Let me be a bit more practical, to illustrate what I mean. My children, when they first read this, will I hope be preparing to set off for a college education. I don't know where they'll go to school. Maybe they'll come to Biola. Maybe they'll head down the street to UC Irvine. Or maybe they'll travel across the country and wind up at the University of Virginia, or Harvard, or MIT, or maybe Grove City College. I don't pretend to know. How will they choose? And when they arrive at these places, they'll face another choice. What major will they choose? English literature, like their mom? Economics, like me as an undergraduate? Philosophy? Mechanical engineering? Theoretical physics? And *how* will they choose? These are obviously highly practical questions: their educational institution and their major will heavily influence the way the rest of their lives unfold, their careers, their circles of influence, maybe if and whom they marry, their deepest friendships.

As they make these decisions—as anyone makes these sorts of decisions—I want them to consider how they are pursuing the fullness of the gospel. Can you conceive of a way that your major will deepen your connection to the grand Creation-Fall-Redemption-

Consummation storyline? Do you see God's hand at work in the spaces you study? In the opportunities that are open to you? In the career path your college experience will establish for you? Does physics make you wonder at God's intellect? Does philosophy help you see the ways God has worked through human thought and culture, or maybe the way sin has warped our minds? Can you imagine your work in business stunting the harm of the Fall? Importantly, this is not the question whether God is in fact at work or visible in these areas. God is at work, and his work is visible, in the whole of creation. These questions are about *you*, not God. What moves *you* into the fullness of the gospel?

Here's a different thing. We live in a chaotic time. Chaotic *intellectually*, I mean. The chaos is, at least in part, prompted by our present "Information Age." Today we have, at our fingertips, more information than our ancestors could have ever imagined. When I was in college, I yearned to have a computer with a 128 MB hard drive. That's 128 *mega*bytes. As I've been writing this book, I've been saving the files on a tiny thumb drive, literally the size of a fingernail, that holds 128 GB of data. Something the size of a fingernail has 1,000 times the capacity of college-me's dream computer. There is so much information that we don't know how to sort it all. And information alone is not knowledge. To turn information into knowledge, we need a way to sort the information, to understand the connections among *this* bit of information and *that* one, and to situate it all into a coherent vision of the world. There is no consensus on how that is supposed to happen, and so our life in community is chaotic and disorienting. As a result, we are prone to retreat into intellectual silos, listening to those we know see the world as we do, or we give ourselves to the ideologies of the powerful, ideologies that are not shaped by the true story of the world. Or, perhaps more often than not, we find ourselves in a silo dominated by an anti-gospel ideology.

In a silo, the trouble is that we hear only echoes of our own voice. Unchallenged, we become convinced that others are either stupid or ignorant. Slowly we begin to treat those with whom we disagree as enemies, and we ourselves become small people with childish minds.

The idea that knowledge is for the love of God, and that what we seek is fullness, gives us a way to tame the chaos of our age. Jesus loves me, this I know, for the Bible tells me so. We already know the storyline. The information we encounter must be taken captive inside this story. We don't need echo chambers. The sorting method we long for is a children's song, and frankly it's a song that no echo chamber sings.

~*~

At the risk of alienating you, dear reader, I want to give this some teeth. Politics, perhaps especially in America, has become a politics of ideology rather than a politics of problem-solving through respectful disagreement and compromise. And I worry that the church is more and more interpreting Christianity through the lens of political ideology rather than politics through Christianity. When we give more attention to politics than to the Scriptures, we train ourselves to think along ideological lines that are not first and foremost about the gospel of Jesus.

Perhaps I ought to be concrete. I know many well-meaning American Christians on both sides of our left-right political divide. Both groups, I believe, sincerely desire justice in their neighborhoods, cities and towns, in the nation as a whole, and even throughout the world. But they disagree (obviously!) about what is required for justice to reign. That disagreement concerns not just the best solutions, but more deeply the specific *contours* of injustice and still more deeply the *roots* of injustice. I'll pick on my friends on the left with respect to contours and my friends on the right with respect to roots. Importantly, these comments are brief. They are meant to spark you to think critically about your own inclinations and to spark conversation. By no means should these words of mine be the last.

I have brothers and sisters on the left who naturally think of justice and injustice as fundamentally about categories like race, ethnicity, sex, gender, and sexual orientation. No doubt injustice along these lines should grieve us all, and there are important reasons to give special attention to, for example, the aftermath of racist policies in our communities. The trouble is that these are not the fundamental categories of the kingdom of God (Gal. 3:26–29). By treating them as fundamental, these well-meaning brothers and sisters often fail to reckon adequately with injustice directed toward other groups. For example, many seem to lack Jesus's profound concern for children, especially unborn children. They—rightly!—feel outrage at the seemingly senseless deaths of Black image bearers at the hands of powerful police officers (who, by the way, are also image bearers). Yet many feel no outrage whatever for the more than two thousand unborn children, many of whom are also Black, that will die on the day you read these words. The idea that the unborn might be among the marginalized simply doesn't occur to them.

On the other hand, I have brothers and sisters on the right who cannot abide the possibility of systemic or community-level evil— evil that is independent of the beliefs and intentions of those presently in the community. When confronted with, for example, racial disparities in academic achievement, income and wealth, or health, these beloved children of God are willing to countenance explanations of the problem and solutions to the problem that deploy individual responsibility, and sometimes even the work of Satan. No doubt the sinful nature and decisions of individual humans, as well as the devil and his minions, wreak havoc in our communities! But the Scriptures teach that we face evil in three forms, not just two

(Matt. 13:1–30, 36–43; Eph. 2:1–3 and 6:12). Theologians have for generations discussed not just the flesh and the devil but also the *world.* These brothers and sisters miss the pernicious contributions of this third dimension of evil. And so the solution they so badly desire remains out of reach.

To be clear, I don't think I've ever met a Christian unconcerned with injustice. My concern is that, increasingly, we are blinded to aspects of injustice by dominant political ideologies. Interestingly, this is one more way that the world, in that theological sense, works on behalf of evil. As Paul instructs the Corinthians (2 Cor. 10:4–5), we must take all our thoughts captive. We must demolish strongholds with the weapons of Christ. For the love of God, we must love God with our minds.

~&

What does it mean, practically, to subject ourselves to the Christian story in the intellectual realm? To think at the foot of the cross? Lots of things. First, it means we seek the truth first. Because all people are made in the image of God, all are capable of accessing the truth. But because of the Fall, we each fail in that endeavor as well. No one person or institution is the sole arbiter of truth. And so we must take the responsibility of inquiry on ourselves, recognizing all the while our own inability to carry this weight perfectly. We must seek truth in community, opening ourselves to the criticisms and insights of others. We must seek truth wherever it can be found, even in the mouths of our enemies. And we must hold our views with the humility appropriate to fallen humanity. This does not mean that we always lack confidence (more on that momentarily). Rather, it means that we are confident to the degree that our evidence is strong. In other words, we are intellectually honest.

Second, inquiry from the foot of the cross is expansive. What I mean is, first, that we are not religiously devoted to any source of evidence other than God alone. We do not fixate on a single voice, whether a pastor or a politician or a blogger or a public intellectual. There is only one infallible voice, and every voice will sometimes get the truth. Even demons know about God and his world. (There are of course far safer people to inquire alongside!) So, for example, if you want to understand the cause of some world crisis, or the roots of some political problem, consult a constellation of voices. If you tend to read the *Wall Street Journal*, pick up a *New York Times*. If you prefer *The Atlantic*, grab an issue of *First Things*. Learn to cull the good and leave behind the bad by examining the way that the "Jesus Loves Me" informs and contextualizes the messages and narratives on those pages.

Third, at the foot of the cross we are compelled to generosity. A central move in contentious conversations is explaining away one's opponent's perspective. We do this by suggesting they are approaching the issue with ulterior motives, but we are not. In this way, we suggest that our intellectual opponents are less rational than we are. This is both false and destructive. We cannot converse with another whom we believe to be operating blindly or in bad faith. We must believe that, by and large, people are honestly pursuing the truth as best they are able. We must refuse to psychologize those with whom we disagree. We are all equally fallen, subject to the intellectual wreckage left in Adam's wake. Listen to the reasons people have for views you deem false, even repulsive or destructive. You just might discover something you had missed. We also endeavor to reveal the truth that has been revealed to us. Not as an attempt to win an argument or show how clever we are, but rather because we know the truth sets a person free. We work to propagate the truth because it matters to our friends and enemies alike.

Along the same path, there is no place for defensiveness at the foot of the cross. Our public discourse is radically defensive. In public spaces, we seem either unwilling or unable to pursue truth and goodness. Instead, we stake our territory and defend it to the death. Defensiveness is inversely proportional to confidence. From the foot of the cross, we are compelled by the radical grace we have received and confronted with the utter security of our futures. We have nothing to fear, and God is capable of defending himself. So we simply investigate. We open ourselves to evidence, and we adjust our beliefs accordingly. We work to believe what we do as confidently as our evidence requires, no more and no less.

~#

If all that sounds demanding, that's because it is. It takes courage to seek the truth no matter what and no matter from where, to generously engage even our enemies, and to avoid defensiveness. How do we gain that sort of courage? I want to make two points about this.

First, to gain intellectual courage, we must have appropriate confidence in the truth of the gospel. Appropriate confidence comes from investigating reality through examining evidence. This is an intellectual task, though one that we've seen is not disconnected from the rest of our hearts. The central claims of Christianity are true. Actually, seriously true. God exists and created everything. Jesus is God's Son. And through him alone are we rescued from the wreckage of sin and death. These are the claims, and there exists all manner of evidence to support them. This evidence is both positive and negative. There are positive reasons to believe God exists, that he is Creator, that Jesus rose from the dead, that by rising from the dead he validated his message, and that his message was that he alone is the path to life with God. And there are other reasons, which might be classified as negative, that deal with objections to all of this. Some of those I've mentioned in prior chapters, to do with whether science is the only path to knowledge (a problem because science may not reveal God's existence, nature, or work) and that religious pluralism should make us doubt our religious convictions. There are amazing resources to consult on these questions, and other questions besides.[3]

Second, to gain intellectual courage, we must encounter stories that display the Truth, in whole or in part. I mentioned previously that C. S. Lewis once said that stories have the power to "steal past ... watchful dragons" in our hearts. What he meant was that stories can break down our defenses, move into our deepest parts, and shape us. The shaping can be good if the stories are good, or bad if the stories are bad. But Lewis's point is simply that stories are powerful shapers of our hearts, including our minds. Fiction helps us glimpse reality, and often that glimpsed reality is more available when situated within a story than it is otherwise.

This is, in fact, a deeply biblical idea. King David needed a story about a stolen, precious sheep, made up by the prophet Nathan and presented as truth, to reveal the horror of his own adultery and murder. Some of Jesus's most iconic teaching is contained within stories, whether about good Samaritans or prodigal sons or demanding bosses. There are, of course, many other examples of this sort of thing recorded in the pages of Scripture. And this model should not be lost on us. I'm obsessed with the *Harry Potter* series. The reason is simple: I think they display some deep, important truths in ways that are far more compelling than when they are simply stated outright. (Spoilers incoming!) Harry's sacrifice of himself on behalf of his friends, and the way that sacrifice protects those friends during the Battle of Hogwarts, shows the protective power of self-giving love. Love is a sort of shield against evil. In the context of *Harry Potter*, we see that shield in a way we cannot observe in the world around us. Or take Solomon, who at the beginning of Proverbs suggests that evil people "lie in wait for their own blood" and "ambush only themselves" (Prov. 1:18). This sounds crazy! Surely the primary victims of evil are, well, the victims! But think about the Unforgivable Curses in *Harry Potter*, from *crucio* to *avada kedavra*. These curses harm those who *use* them, and in many ways this harm is far deeper than those subject to the curse. The killing curse literally tears its user's soul in two, dehumanizing and destroying the killer. The wizard or witch who uses *avada kedavra* ambushes only him- or herself.[4] These examples are just the beginning.

An aside: Nonfiction stories can help us see the unseen too! In chapter 8, we encountered Corrie ten Boom as we wrestled with the seemingly ridiculous things God says through the Bible. On the truth of Proverbs 1, in particular, Frederick Douglass is a witness. Speaking about one of his slavers, Douglass says, "Slavery proved as injurious to her as it did to me. . . . Under its influence, the tender heart [of my mistress] became stone, and the lamblike disposition gave way to one of tiger-like fierceness."[5] Douglass's slaver enslaved herself. Returning to the idea of political ideologies, it's intriguing that both left and right lay claim to great-hearted humans like Douglass. Perhaps both claims are misplaced. Perhaps Douglass was simply a Christian.

I should move on, but I can't help myself! I mean, the whole story of Harry Potter's world is about whether the Order of the Phoenix will prevail over the Death Eaters. The Order of the Phoenix follows the way of the phoenix, the path of the magical bird that embraces its own death with confidence, recognizing that from the ashes of death new life is birthed. Harry, in the end, fully embraces this way. And this is how he becomes the true master of the Deathly Hallows, which he uses to "greet death as a friend" and to at least temporarily conquer it. The Death Eaters, on the other hand, attempt to swallow up death via technological (that is, magical) force. Voldemort is the exemplar of this way. He strives to gain immortality by dismembering his own soul through heinous, repetitive murder. This dichotomy offers a beautiful way to conceive of the difference between the path of Jesus and the path of Satan.

One more. What Hermione needed after Dumbledore's death was something like what I needed in 2006. She had all the knowledge and skill in the world. (That's a difference between her and me, I suppose.) What she didn't know were *The Tales of Beedle the Bard*. Hermione needed children's stories to order her knowledge. She needed to understand how what she already knew wasn't sufficient on its own, and that it was only valuable insofar as it supplies fullness to what she was missing. Hermione needed the wizarding world's equivalent of a Sunday school song.

Harry Potter is not alone in revealing the truth through story. It happens all over the place. You can find truth in the novels of Tolkien and Lewis, in Harper Lee and Shakespeare, in the Marvel Cinematic Universe, and in television shows like *Friday Night Lights* and *Parks and Recreation*. There are even truths embedded in tragic stories like the *Hunger Games*, which reveal the desperation of life in a universe with no overriding storyline. Or in the films of Stanley Kubrick and Darren Aronofsky, who study evil in all its horror. These films aren't for everyone. But each has the power to reveal aspects of the truth to attentive souls. They also have the power to warp us if we let down our guard and embrace them uncritically. God's story is everywhere, and so is human brokenness. Look for hints of the gospel in story, as well as whiffs of evil (which is part of the gospel story as well!). Name the evil and reject it, and embrace the gospel. Let these stories show you both the path to destruction and the narrow path of Jesus.

—✿

Remember, for the love of our Father and his Son our Lord, knowledge is for the love of God.

Chapter 10 Discussion Questions

- At the end of chapter 4, you thought about these questions: Where do you go when you have a question? What sources of information do you trust? A follow-up: What are your go-to sources for information on current events, politics, culture, etc.?
- Who in your life do you let challenge your views? Who will you still listen to even in the midst of disagreement?
- Are there important areas in your life—family, work, politics—that you struggle to connect meaningfully to your Christian faith?
- As you have grown in education and knowledge of the world, have you "ordered it from the foot of the cross"? Or do you approach disciplines without the underpinning narrative of the gospel?
- What have you learned from this book? How will you change the way you learn and study as a result of reading it?

Notes

Chapter 1

1. See, e.g., *Love Your God with All Your Mind: The Role of Reason in the Life of the Soul*, rev. ed. (Colorado Springs: NavPress, 2012). J. P. and William Lane Craig talk about something similar in their *Philosophical Foundations for a Christian Worldview*, 2nd ed. (Downers Grove, IL: IVP Academic, 2017).

2. The University of Texas's original campus covered forty acres; it's now more than ten times that size, but the moniker is still used.

3. This quote is all over the internet but is originally from Chandrashankar Shukla, *Gandhi's View of Life* (Bombay: Bhartiya Vidya Bhavan, 1954), 158.

4. From "Killing the Buddha," *Shambhala Sun*, March 19, 2006. Accessed at samharris.org/killing-the-buddha/; *Shambhala Sun* has since changed its name to *The Lion's Roar* (lionsroar.com). Harris makes similar points in numerous places, maybe most forcefully in his book *The End of Faith: Religion, Terror, and the Future of Reason* (New York: W. W. Norton, 2004).

5. From an interview Stern gave to Camille Paglia for the November 28, 1995, issue of *The Advocate* magazine.

6. *Letter to a Christian Nation* (New York: Vintage Books, 2008), 67.

7. Dennett said this while being interviewed by Bill Moyers on *Charlie Rose* on April 3, 2006.

Chapter 2

1. David Hume, the eighteenth-century Scottish philosopher, is in many ways responsible for providing the philosophical underpinnings of this sort of thing. But that's a subject for a different book.

2. I learned this from my colleague Dave Horner's excellent book, *Mind Your Faith* (Downers Grove, IL: IVP, 2011), 44. He cites H. Wheeler Robinson's "Hebrew Psychology," in *The People of the Book*, ed. Arthur E. Peake (Oxford: Clarendon, 1925). My friend Charlie Trimm, a professor of Old Testament at Biola, confirmed in private correspondence that *lēb* picks out the intellect more often than any other specific faculty. Charlie directed me to the *Theological Dictionary of the Old Testament* for further confirmation.

3. There's actually a third type of knowledge: *know-how*. It's what's involved with knowing how to ride a bike, or how to do the standard algorithm for large number multiplication, or how to build an AT-AT out of Legos, or how to make one's brother laugh when he's being crabby like his dad. I'm going to ignore this kind of knowledge, not because it's not important, but because it's not as important as the others for the purposes of this book.

4. Taken from *Plato: Complete Works*, ed. John M. Cooper, trans. G. M. A. Grube (Indianapolis: Hackett, 1997).

5. Willard offers this definition, or something like it, in a number of places. This is taken from his article "Knowledge and Naturalism," in *Naturalism: A Critical Analysis*, ed. J. P. Moreland and William Lane Craig (New York: Routledge, 2002), 31. He says something similar in *Knowing Christ Today* (New York: HarperCollins, 2009), 71.

Chapter 3

1. Simmons said this in his ESPN Page 2 column on July 9, 2008, two years after that game actually occurred! That column is archived on espn.com: https://www.espn.com/espn/page2/story?page=simmons/060620, accessed August 23, 2021.

2. Russell Shorto, *Descartes' Bones: A Skeletal History of the Conflict between Faith and Reason* (New York: Vintage Books, 2008), 18.

3. René Descartes, *Discourse on Method and the Meditations*, trans. F. E. Sutcliffe (New York: Penguin Books, 1968), 78.

4. Shorto, *Descartes' Bones*, 31.

5. Guinness, *Time for Truth: Living Free in a World of Lies, Hype, and Spin* (Grand Rapids: Baker, 2000), 110.

6. Guinness's *Time for Truth* is a nice little book about this. There are others, including Douglas Groothius, *Truth Decay: Defending Christianity against the Challenges of Postmodernism* (Downers Grove, IL: IVP, 2000), and Paul Boghossian, *Fear of Knowledge: Against Relativism and Constructivism* (Oxford: Oxford University Press, 2006). See also, e.g., J. P. Moreland and William Lane

Craig, *Philosophical Foundations for a Christian Worldview*, 2nd ed. (Downers Grove, IL: IVP Academic, 2017), ch. 6, pp. 118–40.

Chapter 4

1. The story is in Mark 9:14–29.

2. These last few paragraphs pass through a deep, dark forest of interesting and important epistemological questions without really so much as taking notice of the fact that it's a forest, much less deep and dark. I happen to think that the various well-worn paths through the forest all wind one up in a place where you can say what I'm about to say. So I'm not going to bother saying why I choose the particular path that I do.

Chapter 5

1. Luc Ferry, *A Brief History of Thought* (New York: HarperCollins, 2011), 6.

2. Bryan Litfin, *Early Christian Martyr Stories* (Grand Rapids: Baker Academic, 2014), 92.

3. Litfin, *Martyr Stories*, 107.

4. Litfin, *Martyr Stories*, 108–9.

5. Litfin, *Martyr Stories*, 94.

6. John Paul II, *Fides et Ratio* (Boston: Pauline Books, 1998), 45, emphasis mine.

7. It would perhaps be wise to recall Harris's and Dennett's assertions about the irrationality of religion and faith, quoted in chapter 1. They are just flat-out wrong.

Chapter 6

1. Saint Augustine, *City of God*, vol. 1, ed. R. V. G. Tasker, trans. John Healey (London: J. M. Dent & Sons, 1945), 276.

2. *Encounter with God: An Introduction to Chrstian Worship and Practice*, 2nd ed. (London: T&T Clark, 2004), 3.

Chapter 7

1. Richard Dawkins, *The God Delusion* (London: Bantam Press, 2006), 56.

2. See p. 57 of *The God Delusion* for Dawkins's skepticism that theology

ought to count as a subject matter and, e.g., pp. 32 and 34 on the issue of evidence in theology.

3. Dawkins, *God Delusion*, 32.

4. Dawkins, *God Delusion*, 5.

5. Lauren Slater, "True Love," *National Geographic*, February 2006, 35.

6. The text of this letter is widely available. You can find it, for example, on Fordham University's Modern History Sourcebook (https://sourcebooks .fordham.edu/mod/galileo-tuscany.asp) or on the Interdisciplinary Encyclopedia of Religion & Science (http://inters.org/Galilei-Madame-Christina -Lorraine).

7. Arthur Fine, "The Natural Ontological Attitude," in *Philosophy of Science: The Central Issues*, ed. Martin Curd and J. A. Cover (New York: W. W. Norton, 1998), 1194–95; cited by Stokes, *How to Be an Atheist* (Wheaton, IL: Crossway, 2016), 107–8.

8. Fine, "Natural Ontological Attitude," 1195, cited by Stokes, *How to Be an Atheist*, 108.

9. John C. Lennox, *Can Science Explain Everything?* (Epsom, UK: The Good Book Company, 2019), 35.

10. See chapter 7, pp. 77–84, of *Scientism and Secularism: Learning to Respond to a Dangerous Ideology* (Wheaton, IL: Crossway, 2018).

Chapter 8

1. *A Grief Observed* (New York: HarperOne, 2000), 5–6.

2. Lewis, *Grief*, 6–7.

3. Three of my favorites are Timothy Keller, *The Reason for God* (New York: Penguin Books, 2008); Dan Kimball, *How (Not) to Read the Bible* (Grand Rapids: Zondervan, 2020); and Rebecca McLaughlin, *Confronting Christianity* (Wheaton, IL: Crossway, 2019). There are more!

4. Exposition on Psalm 64 (which is Psalm 65 in modern, Protestant English Bibles). Older editions of Augustine's commentaries on the Psalms are public domain, so you can find them online in lots of places, including the Internet Archive (archive.org). Maria Boulding's is the translation with which I am most familiar, though it is not public domain. The exposition on Psalm 64 is found in *Expositions on the Psalms 51–72*, vol. III/17, trans. Maria Boulding, in *The Works of Saint Augustine: A Translation for the 21st Century*, ed. John E. Rotelle (Hyde Park, NY: New City Press, 2001). See p. 267 for Augustine's claim that "our Father has sent us letters." The next sentence gives God's reason: "God has provided the scriptures for us, so that by these letters from him our longing to return home may be aroused."

5. *The Collected Letters of C. S. Lewis*, vol. 3: *Narnia, Cambridge, and Joy 1950–1963*, ed. Walter Hooper (New York: HarperCollins, 2007), 354.

6. *Collected Letters of C. S. Lewis*, 3:356.

7. If you're interested in the sort of defense I'm not giving, there is a veritable host of resources to engage about all manner of questions and issues related to the truth of Christianity and the nature of the Bible. I'd encourage you to start with something like Lee Strobel's *Case for Christ* (Grand Rapids: Zondervan, 1998), and its siblings in the *Case for* series. These books are great all on their own, but they also introduce you to excellent thinkers to grapple with as you go forward. You can also reach out to me directly, about this or anything else, through my website: pancakevictim.org.

8. *The Hiding Place* (Grand Rapids: Chosen Books, 2006); Corrie ten Boom's *Prison Letters* (Fort Washington, PA: CLC Publications, 2015).

9. Jim Belcher, *In Search of Deep Faith: A Pilgrimage into the Beauty, Goodness and Heart of Christianity* (Downers Grove, IL: InterVarsity Press, 2013); Eric Metaxas, *Seven Women: And the Secret of Their Greatness* (Nashville: Nelson Books, 2015). Please just ignore the introduction of Metaxas's book, though, which bizarrely suggests that traits like innocence, purity, holiness, and vulnerability are somehow distinctively feminine and "unmanly." No doubt Metaxas meant well with these comments, but they manage rather miraculously to exemplify benevolent sexism while also insinuating, insultingly, that real men can't be innocent, pure, holy, and vulnerable. You can see this sort of thing on p. xv, as Metaxas describes how Joan of Arc's accomplishments are rooted in her "singularity as [a woman]" and then explains that singularity by talking about purity and holiness and such. Jesus would no doubt be surprised to find these ought to stand in tension with genuine manhood.

10. Ten Boom, *Hiding Place*, 191–92.

11. Ten Boom, *Hiding Place*, 192.

12. Ten Boom, *Hiding Place*, 210.

13. Ten Boom, *Hiding Place*, 222.

14. Ten Boom, *Hiding Place*, 220.

15. Carl Trueman's *The Rise and Triumph of the Modern Self: Cultural Amnesia, Expressive Individualism, and the Road to Sexual Revolution* (Wheaton, IL: Crossway, 2020) is a profoundly helpful partial history of this progression. Readers attentive to both Trueman and this book will notice that I think we need to trace the history still further back than Trueman endeavors to do in that book. (I suspect he would agree! Every book has its boundaries.)

16. He said this in "Sometimes Fairy Stories May Say Best What's to Be Said." This essay appears in Lewis's *On Stories: And Other Essays on Literature* (New York: Harvest Books, 1982).

Chapter 9

1. Kelly Kapic, *Embodied Hope: A Theological Meditation on Pain and Suffering* (Downers Grove, IL: IVP Academic, 2017), 24.

2. Frederickson has published widely about this. There's even a Wikipedia page about her theory: wikipedia.org/wiki/Broaden-and-build. But you can read her work in serious scholarly outlets as well. As an example, you might check out her paper "The Value of Posivite Emotions," *American Scientist* 91, no. 4 (2003): 330–35, or her paper "The Broaden-and-Build Theory of Positive Emotions," *Philosophical Transactions of the Royal Society B: Biological Sciences* 359, no. 1449 (2004): 1367–78. The points I'll make shortly about negative emotions aren't Frederickson's, but they are perhaps even more widely established and accepted.

3. I actually think there are deeper, more subtle ways that emotions shape knowledge. But my views are somewhat controversial, so I'm sticking with a more obvious connection between emotions and knowledge for the time being.

4. I don't mean to suggest that fear of falling off a cliff and divine fear are totally alike! But they do share certain things in common. In particular, I'm concerned with that aspect of all fear that is connected to the recognition of danger. It is a dangerous thing to come into God's presence. The danger is different than that of a cliff. And God has of course made it possible for us to enter into his presence without harm. God's presence is dangerous nonetheless. The fear of God really is *fear*.

Chapter 10

1. Thanks to Liz Hall for pointing me to this passage.

2. Bavinck, *The Doctrine of God*, trans. William Henrickson (Grand Rapids: Eerdmans, 1951), 329.

3. Some suggestions on where to begin, leaving out what I've already mentioned (see esp. n. 3 of chapter 8): Greg Ganssle, *Our Deepest Desires* (Downers Grove, IL: IVP Academic, 2017); Michael Rota, *Taking Pascal's Wager* (Downers Grove, IL: IVP Academic, 2016). There are more like these! That's not to mention all the great podcasts, video content, and so on. As I mentioned in an earlier footnote, feel free to reach out to me at my website, pancakevictim .org. I'm happy to offer guidance!

4. This highlights the tragedy of Snape. Snape agreed to embrace this sort of evil as an act of mercy toward both Dumbledore and Draco Malfoy. Whether it makes Snape morally heroic is a separate, thorny question.

5. *Narrative of the Life of Frederick Douglass* (Mineola, NY: Dover, 1995), 22.

Index

Augustine, 77, 106
Bachelorette, The, 17–19, 114
Barth, Karl, 138–40
Bavinck, Herman, 141
belief, 10, 11, 24–25, 30, 43, 50
  and action, 55–56, 66
  content of, 46–47
  as mental map, 48
  nature of, 45–48
  propositional, 50
  reasonable, 24, 25, 43, 45, 47–49,
    54, 69, 128
  and unbelief, 41–43, 45, 57
  See also faith, as belief in; rational-
    ity: of belief
Bible, 7, 20, 27, 54, 72, 75, 79, 104,
  108, 117, 142
  authority of, 92, 105
  primacy of, 105
  as testimony, 123
  See also Scripture
Bohr, Niels, 95
Chicago Cubs, 43
Christian story, four-part, 129–30,
  137–38, 141, 143–44
communion with God, 77–78

constructivism. *See* truth:
  constructivism about
Copernicus, Nicolaus, 33, 34
courage, intellectual, 149
Creation-Fall-Redemption
  Consummation narrative. *See*
  Christian story, four-part
culture, 8–9, 19, 20, 54, 107
Darwin, Charles, 36, 93
Dawkins, Richard, 88, 89, 92, 97
Dennett, Daniel, 9, 17
Descartes, René, 34–36
disagreement, 72, 120, 123, 129
  as evidence, 125
  rational response to, 124–25
  See also pluralism
divine testimony, 115
Douglass, Frederick, 151
education, 54, 57
education versus manipulation,
  42, 45
Edwards, Jonathan, 126
Einstein, Albert, 95
emotions, 20, 115, 129
  and evidence, 128
  and intellect, 126
  negative, 127